CW01624230

SIGNALS FROM ETERNITY

The Autobiography of a 20th Century Mystic

Books by Kate Thomas

SIGNALS FROM ETERNITY Volume I of a Trilogy

Part 1 *Intimations*

Part 2 *Framework for Tuition*

Part 3 *Approach to the Teacher*

BELOVED EXECUTIONER Volume II

Part 1 *The Teacher*
(Life in the midst of death)

Part 2 *The Test*
(Death in the midst of life)

Appendix

A CHARTED DESTINY Volume III

Part 1 *Route of Return*

Part 2 *Subterranean Descent*

Part 3 *Gateway to Eternity*

SIGNALS FROM ETERNITY

The Autobiography of a 20th Century Mystic

KATE THOMAS

ROSEKING PUBLICATIONS

Copyright 1984 by Kate Thomas
First impression in this Edition 1984
Second impression 1986

Hardback: ISBN 0 946402 03 5

All rights of reproduction and translation are reserved

No part of this publication may be reproduced in any form or by any means without prior permission obtained in writing from the publishers of this book.

Printed in Great Britain by
Redwood Burn Limited, Trowbridge, Wiltshire

Cover: Jill Wood.
Photoset in England by The Granta Press, Cambridge
Published by ROSEKING PUBLICATIONS,
P.O. Box 13. CAMBRIDGE CB4 1EZ ENGLAND.

This is a true story. Much has been left out, for as in any life the greater part is incommunicable, and thoughts, feelings, joys and fears, events and conversations, can only be hinted at, or approximations. In the last analysis we must each live out our own experience in all its solitariness.

Yet some lives have a pattern — perhaps a destiny, and the shaping of this in words, even as an understatement, can convey to fellow travellers a glimpse of a hidden Reality — charting a further track homewards to that Unknown and largely forgotten country from which we set out.

Author's Note.

Readers may observe that each book in this autobiographical series is written in a different style. This was not intentional and is simply the result of reliving in retrospect events and experiences of long ago, and recounting them in accord with situations and viewpoints then current; plus the incorporation of existing notes from the appropriate period. For this reason the entire record has been separated into three sections, reflecting as adequately as possible the changes that occurred as the link between spirit and personality grew stronger.

K. W. T.

CONTENTS

To my son and daughter

With love

PART 1

INTIMATIONS

Man does not have it in him
to desire things the like of which
have been prepared for him.

Hakim Sanai: 'The Walled Garden of Truth'
translated by David Pendlebury,
Octagon Press Ltd. 1974 p. 24.

From the very beginning I believed that something wonderful would one day happen — I did not know what, or how, but my earliest, clearly conscious recollection, is a swift mental picture of running joyously into the world, through buttercup meadows, to meet someone very dearly loved.

When I was five, and playing in a sunny field sprinkled with buttercups and daisies, I had a sudden brief memory of this — a transient moment of awareness that filled me with a strange longing and an aftermath of fear, for I could not understand either this, or the narrow limits of my childish mentation.

I was born in the May of 1928, on the twenty-second day, during a thunderstorm. A first child, I arrived in my aunt's country cottage in Cherryhinton, Cambridgeshire, to young, penniless and hardworking parents who, if they had to have a child at all, would wish it to be a boy. Fortunately for me, they overcame their disappointment, and I was well loved.

My memories reach right back into babyhood. I recall lying quietly on a bed between my parents, and my father getting up to dress and stubbing his toe, swearing strongly. The words most certainly were the first sharp ones I heard, and shocked me into vivid perception. The room was described to my mother in later years, and was one from which we moved before I was nine months old.

Other glimpses emerge, of little consequence, but registering an increasing grasp of 'self'. Life was all very frightening; I was a little spark of feeling and observation, locked in a dark, lonely place, and as I grew my mind repeatedly pondered on *how* I was here, and where I had come from. When I was five I had my tonsils removed, and this proved a traumatic experience which affected me afterwards for years. I was unable to swiftly lose consciousness under the anaesthetic, and screamed in terror as four white-coated individuals held me down, one to each limb, and forcibly administered it by mask. Everything gradually faded out, yet still I *was* — I existed in a strange interim state, observing a white-robed, feminine Being stationed above the nucleus that was 'I', who in some manner centralised my consciousness and restored calm.

This happened a second time six months later. I was given dental gas, and struggled wildly again beneath the mask, to soon blank out as far as the world was concerned, but remaining conscious in the dark until I fell from the large dental chair, and awoke.

My brother was born just before I was six, and though I registered, without comprehending, that I now took 'second place', the adored boy was also adored by *me.* He was a lovely child, gentle and rosy and handsome; generally admired, but so goodnatured and most obviously delighting in his older sister, that I was never jealous of him. I remember my grandmother's indiscreet comment on how unalike we were, "one so pretty, the other so plain". This, and other remarks through the years, caused me to know my place, and my total lack of significance in the scheme of things.

But I was clever at school, as my teachers consistently reported. My father, a self-employed tradesman, was naturally pleased. It was a pity indeed I was only a girl, such a waste of good brains... it was, of course, the son that was destined to shine and eventually inherit the slowly prospering business. In my father's world, the only conceivable destiny for a daughter was marriage.

My later scholarships were not encouraged, and my grammar-school place not taken. I attended a scholarship-entry school but of the commercial variety. The headmistress, however, was an old Girtonian as were others of her staff, and their nurturing of myself towards this end was ultimately and calamitously undone by Father's arbitrary removal of me from school at the earliest possible date to earn my own living. There was no thought of a career, or choice of employment. He placed me at once as a clerk in a corn chandler's office, and I did not know for many, many years what this hasty, and strongly opposed (by my teachers) action had cost me.

Nevertheless, long before this came other events which stand out like signposts in my memory, and pointed the way to a process of learning not requiring the Oxbridge tuition I was so firmly denied. An early indication arose on the day we moved into the detached, Victorian house that remained the parental home ever after. I was almost seven, and still recall the sheer delight of the old, unkempt garden with its little brick paths flanked with purple irises, and the massed, unruly clumps of tulips and early bluebells that spread in neglected glory beneath the ancient apple trees. Visually I absorbed their wondrous and colourful profusion, inhaling the damp, clear odours of spring, my senses suddenly acute, and my whole being intensely aware. There was a moment of absolute quietude — a stillness penetrating deep inside me and linking with that other memory of running, running, and such joy... This brief experience left its trace in me throughout my life, while textbooks of studious thought entered and exited my mind quite meaninglessly, and whole chunks of time in terms of days and weeks and months, disappeared entirely.

I attended a Church school — St. Augustine's, and later, at eight, St. Luke's, a junior school for girls only. I was increasingly happy there and enjoyed the lessons, reading avidly everything I could find. From the second year onwards I took the lead in school plays, and in my last term wrote, produced, and acted in my own, courageously asking our amazed Vicar if it was possible for me to hire the Church Hall for a properly staged repetition. Gravely he replied it would cost eighteen shillings, a sum I tried hard to raise, but without success.

Yet despite this confidence in a particular sphere, I was a shy, retiring child, obedient and cautious — my exuberance and initiative manifesting largely in drama and games. I loved other children but was nervous of the bigger, assertive ones, and much afraid of the roughness of boys. I was afraid, too, of war, and long before it broke out, prayed nightly to God to prevent it. When Neville Chamberlain gave his famous "Peace in our time" speech in 1938, something inside me remained undeceived, and continued in dread amidst the rejoicing.

Another phenomenon, almost subliminal, disturbed my days — an inner wailing fraught with grief assailed intangibly my inward ear. In later, adult years I heard it again, and learned then what it signified. My heart seemed to overturn as a television documentary portrayed the persecution of the Jews, backed by a soundtrack of their traditional Judaic lament.

Although I did not realise it I was psychic from childhood, aware of subtleties and undercurrents, the depressions of adults, and whether people liked me or not. I dreamed frequently and vividly, projecting impressions to such an extent that bedtime was sometimes alarming, and sleep a questionable benefit to be deferred as long as possible.

At five I saw my first film — which petrified me though I could not articulate this. The story (fictitious) was of a secret invention of sonic beams that destroyed aircraft — bringing the awareness of unseen destructive forces to the forefront of my consciousness. The stark terror experienced is interesting to me now, for it denoted the fact that even then I was subconsciously aware of the major occult event that would in due time confront me.

My mother took me, at eight years old, to see a film set in Elizabethan England. This was my second visit to the cinema, and it sparked off a series of terrifying nightmares in which I, too, was living in Tudor times, in constant fear of execution. Other dreams were of a recurrent massacre in a temple, and a time spent with gypsies, plus a sleep-perception of the exquisite hand-dances of India, to name but a few — all of course entirely unlinked to my external life and understanding.

My first extrasensory experience intruded into life around now, at the age of nine. I was calling my mother one morning as I leaned over the upstairs bannisters and she was walking below. Suddenly, for a crystal-clear moment, to my frightened eyes she appeared as a short, familiar figure in a brown monk's habit, with a wooden object and a heavy key hanging from a tasselled girdle. Shocked and afraid, I registered that here was my mother, yet at the same time this monklike person who had held authority over me and caused me to suffer terribly. I did not know what to do with this perception, which, like all else experienced in this way, was unvoiced. I had no knowledge then of reincarnation, no means by which to measure it, and did my best to eradicate it from my mind.

At ten I began to write poetry, and continued to do this until my marriage. I also wrote plays and short stories; painted and sketched. I read prodigiously, yet was as athletic as a boy, running, long-jumping, cartwheeling etc., and well able to stand up for myself in occasional battles with contemporaries. Fencing fascinated me, as did anything requiring quick, skilled movement. My untutored efforts lacked grace, and included tap and ballet dancing and a slavish emulation of the romantic waltz and polka seen in films.

The war and adolescence changed a lot of things. I turned away from athletic pursuits and immersed myself in classical literature and in serious attempts to express on paper the expanding depth of my thoughts. This held in check the upwelling fear that stemmed from a constant awareness of pain and violent death. I could not understand the calm acceptance of world conflict on the part of my schoolfriends, who seemed not to feel the continual terror inherent in air-raids; for even if we ourselves did not get the bombs transported in throbbing loads overhead, someone did. Nor did they appear conscious of the ghastly fate of the Jews in concentration camps, or of the agonies of the front line. My mother, too, was ultra sensitive to the war, and her unspoken fear and heartache combined with my own to create a formidable burden.

At last it was over, and the sense of joy and thanksgiving that rose in me as I cycled through the bunting-hung streets, brilliant with flags, has never been forgotten. I was just sixteen, and life took on a new freedom and changed its pattern accordingly.

Already I had learned the bliss of solitude, and during the previous year had covered the immediate countryside on my own, entranced by the pretty villages. The colours of nature were absorbed like wine — I adored the flamelike tints of autumn and revelled in blurred mists and soft rain. I sensed the pregnant surge that underlay the stark beauty of winter, and felt the sap rise in the earth at the coming of spring — I watched it emerge in a teaming wonder of blossom, and heard it in the passionate song of birds. In the midst of the burgeoning trees was a potent stillness charged with creative force — which plucked in me a reciprocal chord of rapture. I drew... and painted... and wrote.

On leaving school, at my mother's instigation I had joined the Methodist Youthclub, and soon found great pleasure in the drama productions and regular debates. The minister took me under his wing, I'm not sure why, but perhaps because he discovered I wrote poetry, and he later encouraged me to read aloud some pieces on the war. Looking back, I can see I was quite a duality — yet my solitary, mystical leanings never seemed at variance with the other traits which now rapidly emerged. I began to observe with amazement the state of suppression and subordination in which my mother and countless other women lived, and became as a consequence fiercely socialist, moralist, and suffragette. My viewpoint was largely Victorian, having been fed on Louisa M. Alcott, Charles Dickens, Emily Bronte and the rest; but basically it was an innate idealism that caused my abhorrence of double standards, nurtured effectively by the reasons I saw for the extinction of joyful love which seemed to occur on entering into the tyranny of matrimony.

I was a natural firebrand. I saw too much and was too forthright. I spoke out once from the rostrum of a village church against the previously voiced, rigidly narrow prejudices of its members, and made my point by unargueably quoting Jesus. Our minister sat beside me in the homeward coach scarcely able to conceal his laughter; but he taught me not to baldly state the truth as I saw it, even if it *was* true, because of its shattering effect, and in many small ways helped me to come to terms with the unyielding sounding-board inside me and the blind hypocrisy I found at every turn.

Even so, my views were very lopsided. I did not then understand the subtle domination of men by women, and by what means — nor how this caused so many backfirings. And ironically, it never occurred to me that my own marriage, if and when it came, could ever bring me anything but bliss.

In my sixteenth year I fell in love. The boy concerned was employed by the same firm as myself, but as a van driver and deliverer of goods. Scholastically we were poles apart, but I was quite oblivious of such matters and knew only that he was intelligent, handsome, lively and kind. An aura of shock enveloped him, and this was what first attracted me. He had been in the London bombing and was rescued from his ruined home — dug out from the rubble — and still suffered the aftermath. We had a delightful companionship for some months, trailing through the countryside together and sitting in cinemas when the nights grew chill.

My mother, watching her one ewe lamb like a hawk, surprisingly allowed me to wander freely that summer; but she told me long afterwards she had felt intuitively I was safe with him, and in a town swarming with troops of all nationalities regarded him as a blessing.

This enchanted idyll was not to last, for soon conscription claimed him, and it was not long before he found a far more experienced and cooperative love than mine. His departure from my life was like a bereavement — devastatingly sudden and very painful emotionally; but with youthful resilience I soon overcame the effects, and for around a year went to dances and involved myself with various young men, two of whom proposed marriage — though I did not feel deeply enough about either to accept.

Much as I loved dancing there were still bleak moments. I withdrew one evening from the swirling throng, suddenly disturbed by the artificiality I saw all about me. Staring unhappily at myself in the cloakroom mirror, on impulse I wiped away every trace of the light make-up I wore, and walked home alone through the dark, silent streets. I can still remember that sad, lost feeling, and the inexplicable sense of isolation — like that of a stranger in an unknown land.

Several months later I met the young airman who was to become my husband. It was June, and I was now nineteen and Patrick was four years older. He was Yorkshire born and bred, of Irish descent, lively yet fundamentally serious... of medium height with dark wavy hair — unusually handsome. He was also a drinker, but this I neither grasped nor recognised. Just back from Burma, he too, had an aura of tragedy which for me eclipsed all else. The attraction between us was instant and mutual, and suddenly and completely my life moved into a different phase.

Reverting back now to my fifteenth year, I discovered at this time my ability to foresee the future — not in its entirety of course, but in brief flashes that gave insight into certain events. At first this aptitude was registered with pleasure, but I quickly found it would not prove a comfortable acquisition and soon grew wary of utilising it. The awareness of this precognitive faculty burst in upon me in several ways; in dreams; by telepathic experience, and through reading a book on palmistry. Through the latter I found that I could read palms effortlessly — not so much by studying their lines, though these were followed visually, but by focussing my attention at a point behind the centre of my forehead. Prognostications, both expressed and unexpressed, proved so accurate that I became alarmed. This relentless faculty was like a double-edged sword, revealing both good and bad with equal impartiality. The 'good' I could take in my stride, but the reverse filled me with foreboding. After seeing serious illness ahead for my mother (on which I remained silent), I ceased my activities in this field and no longer tried to probe forming events. But in due time the illness came, with such severity that it altered the previous trend of my mother's life and changed her outlook entirely.

The telepathic experience was emotionally less charged; one afternoon when working in the office, I saw suddenly flashed on some interior screen at the back of my eyes, the replica of a brooch given me two years previously by a friend. This brooch had been lost within a very short time of receiving it, and subsequently forgotten. To my surprise, on my return home my mother produced the brooch, which had been found beneath debris in the garden at the same hour I had seen it in my head.

In dreams too, came foreshadowings of the future; but more important to me than any of these was a link with my destiny, and at sixteen I had an extraordinarily vivid experience in sleep which appeared to stem from another dimension. The stratum of life it revealed was undoubtedly symbolic, as whatever I registered had to be translated through my brain with all its conditioned limitations, but it was the first *remembered* contact with the shining, white robed Being I later knew as my Teacher.

It seemed I was taken into the caverns beneath the surface of the earth, and there left on my own to talk with the inhabitants. They were rough, crude people, wearing skins, and I was very frightened. I began to tell them of the life of Christ, who had once lived among them — and for a while they listened, but soon grew restless and angry. From their midst I took a small child and held him in my arms — for his removal seemed the purpose of my mission; and when they realised I meant to take him away with me, they closed in with threatening, violent gestures. Terrified now, and still clasping the child, I raised a jewelled cross above my head, and willed with all my strength that my Companion should return. Silently, from my heart I summoned him — "Father... Father... Father...", and swiftly and silently he came. We moved rapidly from that place on winged feet, by a process of levitation — our feet were motionless, with tiny, pulsating wings of flame at the heels, and we travelled with speed about a foot from the ground.

On waking I was filled with wonder — for he whom I called Father, I *knew*. He alone was Real in a world of shadows, and this I recognised and cherished, without any understanding of its portent.

There were other curious experiences — of moving purposefully through mist, and remonstrating with, or consoling, the people I found there. I remember a woman who stood on a bridge and repeatedly committed suicide by throwing herself off into the water below. She appeared to be trapped in a recurring pattern, unable now to change it through following for too long the line of least resistance. I had been sent to disentangle her fixed impressions, or responses, and thus enable her to gain release for herself.

On another occasion, I spoke to a woman who had disobeyed a law, or ruling, and had left herself psychically open to the entry of (or possession by) an undeveloped elemental force that she had once tried to enslave. This was commanded from her, not without difficulty, and some form of treatment and instruction given to prevent it happening again. Her location was a small hill, symbolically reflecting her higher level of ability than that of the mass — which had been misused. The penalties for such abuse are severe, in that the undoing of the results of these defiances inevitably brings great distress to the doer.

A man likewise was firmly bound in a certain manner to an oak tree, to prevent an aspect of himself manifesting in life and causing disruption. Through this, he would 'grow round' his weak point, and in time cancel it out altogether with the strengthening of finer qualities.

Many experiences faded rapidly from my mind as I awoke; they were connected with a process of training, and in each instance I was left alone to carry out a function already taught. At these times I wore a white garment, and was utterly dedicated to the task in hand.

At the age of eighteen and a half, I was taken in sleep to meet my future husband. We both 'wore' bodies of the same subtle substance, and floated effortlessly in a leafy glade. His eyes were closed and he was quite unconscious of my presence. The One who took me on this journey conveyed to me the details of my coming marriage, giving some counsel and instruction concerning it; but on waking, although the visual memory remained, the relevant information had been completely eradicated from my awareness. In June, just six months later, I met Patrick.

We both knew, almost from the start, that we would marry — though marriage had certainly not been his intention — he had thought to remain single and free. When he realised how deeply he felt, he tried quite ruthlessly to break away — but the attraction was too strong; and with my watchful mother and equally alert father, there was no other way for him to involve himself with me but by marriage.

The traits that were later to prove so arduous were all held before me during the nine months I knew him, but I was quite blind to their implications. It was as if I was blinkered. And much as I loved him I wasn't quite sure about early marriage, and sought to defer it despite my pleasure at becoming engaged. He and my mother, however, unwittingly combined, for quite different reasons, to bring it about — and it all 'just happened' without any real volition of my own. I awoke feeling ill on my wedding day and longed to cancel it, but arrangements were too far gone and it would upset too many people. The following day I collapsed with a kidney germ, and spent my honeymoon in bed on doctors orders, too ill to get out of it. Fortunately there had been no plans for going away.

We set up house in two upstairs rooms in my parents home. Patrick had been demobilised in November, and had privately decided his own home town in the Industrial North of England was unsuitable for his future bride — he had therefore taken work with my father as a trainee builder (the polite term for labourer), and the wages were commensurate. Prior to our marriage he had frequently taken me dancing, and listened with apparent interest to my poetic meanderings and intuitive perceptions; but with matrimony I learned, came maturity, and it was time for all such frivolities to cease. Intellectually, he was more than my equal, but stemming from the impoverished working classes had, like myself, been obliged to forego his scholastic opportunities, in his case to help support younger brothers and sisters. His 'bent' was political in essence, and his views were left-wing socialist and agnostic — though perhaps atheist would be a more apt word. Poetry, painting, novel-writing — all to him were untasted and undesirable interests as I now discovered, and regarded as pointless superfluities in the life of the spouse of a working man. Likewise a public house was the only proper place for relaxation, and, verging on twenty, I soon understood that my dancing days were over.

My shocked discernment of these facts precipitated our first discord, which rapidly cleared the air of many illusions, and I knew then beyond doubt that to persevere in my former ways would provoke constant and destructive conflict. I dimly grasped through the veils of my own conditioning that his concepts were unaccountably different from mine, and it took time to perceive the environmental and hereditary codes that had formed them.

Less blind now, yet still loving him, I tried to please — endeavouring at the same time to conceal from my parents, and from myself, the alarming extent of my rude awakening to the realities of existence.

I soon sought refuge in maternity, the only route open to me, fixing my mind on the thought of a child. My first baby miscarried, to my great grief, but my son arrived just after my twenty-second birthday. The months I carried him were, I believe, the happiest of my married life.

Pregnancy was a revelation to me — a minor miracle. As each day I felt the baby's movements grow stronger, repeatedly the lovely words of the Chinese women came to me — "I have happiness within me". Gradually I handmade a complete layette, with edgings of lace and embroidery, and trimmed a wicker cradle with pink satin and ribbons — not because I wanted a girl, but to make her 'welcome'. Eventually my robust son asserted his maleness amongst the pink frills, and wore his lacy pink cardigans with masculine aplomb. I adored him.

Throughout my pregnancy Patrick was kind and considerate, and walked the floor in the traditional manner during my lengthy labour. But the baby — beautiful, big, and dynamically energetic, needed little sleep himself, and ensured that his parents got even less of such indulgences. He roared seemingly without cease, and after a few weeks of pride in his offspring, Patrick stated bluntly that he wished we hadn't had him. And he truly meant it. He got very drunk to prove it, and my world again shattered with frightening ease during the days which followed.

This time I picked up the pieces. Hard work though the baby was (and he was an absolute tyrant!) I never once regretted his birth. Patrick worked all hours to avoid the bedlam, but I set about knitting together our lives and establishing a workable pattern. Virtually overnight I grew up, and accepted responsibility for steering the course of this unstable craft, our marriage — as otherwise, I knew, despite the mutual and genuine love, it would soon capsize — and I acknowledged somewhere within myself that it was required to continue.

Two months before my wedding day, my grandfather died. He had lived with us for ten years and I was very fond of him. He was a person who saw much but said little, and had always championed me as a child, taking great interest in my efforts at playwriting and production. Several weeks before his passing, I dreamed of a pale sickle moon set high in a tranquil sky. A few days later he had a stroke, and then a second one, and within a fortnight had passed peacefully away.

I had known intuitively my dream was a portent of death, and some months later with great misgiving saw the same sign again, but this time close to the earth, large and full, and tinged with red. In less than two weeks a young friend died tragically of tuberculosis. This dream repeated almost identically in eighteen months time, and Patrick's younger sister died of the same illness although it had been believed she was recovering. Later still I dreamt of the swift eclipse of a small, silver, high-set moon located directly above a certain point in the nearest cemetery, and within three weeks my grandmother suffered a sudden stroke, and in a span of days had gone from us. Her passing was radiant. The aunts in attendance (her two eldest daughters) reported that she surfaced from unconsciousness "before the end" and spoke happily of the long-dead relations coming to greet her. She was buried incidentally at the spot I had seen, which had no former connection with our family.

In the personal symbolism of dreams the moon to me obviously signified a passing; but any sign in the sky other than the moon I learned to distinguish as a warning of severance — the end of friendships or connections, either permanently, or for a period of time.

My attention was by this means drawn to the study of images projected in sleep, and how they related to the life events that followed. I noted that patterns of images reflected again and again, conveying information that could, with careful observation, be made intelligible. Individual symbols carried similar attributes, and the brief interlude between sleeping and waking was a fruitful source of such material. I eventually linked the perception of pearls with tears, of black grapes with sickness; small coins with minor change, a hatching egg for new events, bread for significant information, a stormy sea for distress etc. An interesting point is that these symbolic foreshadowings were always of matters outside my control; there was no way that I could alter them. They entered my life through the media of others and were either emotionally undeflectable or physically 'fixed'.

Some intimations of death appeared to involve a type of telepathy. One night when an uncle lay seriously ill, I was wakened by a gentle voice against my ear saying quietly, "He's gone. Ethel's with him". It was three o'clock in the morning — the exact time he died. Ethel was his dearly loved first wife.

Another time I awoke in panic to hear a plane whine overhead, and heard it dive, completely out of control. I found myself clutching my stomach with frenzied hands, so tightly they hurt, crying "My God, my God" — and then heard the crash. The boy pilot, just nineteen, was killed, and I truly believe I tuned into his last terrified moments.

One aspect that puzzled me concerned 'visiting' in sleep those who had died. They appeared to be going backwards in time, and grew younger, but noticed nothing strange in my remaining as they had known me last. One older friend was contacted periodically for several years, and went back steadily through her life bit by bit until she arrived at the period when her grown-up children were tiny — this being the last time I saw her. I realise now they were assimilating their lifetime's experiences.

It is difficult to comment briefly on these incidents. They are akin to those found in spiritualism, and well attested, though less well understood. Similar perceptions have brought comfort to many people and the conviction of some form of continued existence after death; yet in essence all were fundamentally different to the training episodes, which appeared to arise from quite another source.

Most of the psychic insights that occurred spontaneously throughout those years were quite trivial and of little importance. They, and the many remembered dreams, simply served to attune my awareness to their varying vibratory levels, and through a long process of observation I gradually learned to discern the wheat from the chaff.

My mundane life now swung over in its entirety to domesticity, but the intermittent other-dimensional enlightenment continued as before, and many times my white-robed Companion led me through the starry Universe and showed me strange scenes, only part-recalled. I also glimpsed fragments of what I felt to be former lives, though I could not grasp *how* this was possible; and whatever I registered regarding these could be seen to have some subtle link with this one.

Yet the effect of such perceptions was small. It was as if I was only partially awake, sensing subconsciously each forward step in time, and gathering impressions and odd snippets of information which were woefully incomplete. I knew I received instruction — and admonition, but have no recollection at all of praise — though sometimes I would waken with a sense of deep happiness that had nothing whatever to do with my daily life, which grew increasingly difficult.

My mother's precognised illness had covered a several year period and culminated in a major operation. As a direct consequence, and pending the imminent surgery, she marshalled all her courage and resolved to do what she had long wished for years, namely, attend a Christian Spiritualist Church. I watched, appalled, one afternoon when she approached my father to acquaint him with this fact, her voice trembling with nervousness. There is no doubt at all that he loved her — she was the central pivot of his life, yet the orphaned girl she had been was readily shaped by 'duty', and all her own hopes and wishes had been foregone through the years to please or placate him. Though a good and honourable man, my father's mind was closed to all else save the world in which he lived.

It seemed to me a travesty of love that she should have to stand there before him, like a criminal before a judge, imploring the right to do, without his recrimination, something that meant so very much to her; particularly now, as she faced the narrow divide between major surgery and death. It was, after all, simply to visit a church whose sole function was to preach survival — the continuity of life. My heart ached for her with the burning pity of youth, and I little knew my own crisis of spiritual decision, wrought in a much sterner mould, lay concealed far off in the future.

Having achieved her aim with the emotional impetus of the operation, Mother tenuously survived it, and with the steady return to health reshaped her outlook totally. This inevitably created problems between my parents and ultimately tipped the balance of power — but the external change commenced slowly and showed itself, for quite a long period, solely to me.

Mother had always been ultra-sensitive and devout, a heritage from her well-bred origins, and the Christian Spiritualists soon recognised in her a natural medium. She attended classes, made bosom friends, and became eventually a healer, speaker and clairvoyant. I listened with absorbed interest to all that transpired — debarred from these activities, of course, by my baby, as most meetings and classes were held in the afternoons; though evenings were equally impossible, for Patrick firmly declined to ever stay in and look after him.

I had always been deeply attached to my mother, but her new career and certain friendships now subtly caused a rift between us, unvoiced but perceptible. Her normal severity of manner increased with her status, and she was quick to correct and advise me — the only member of her family to whom she could speak on such matters — with the unassailable wisdom of her 'guides'. These uncomfortable impartations seldom originated from herself, but were passed to her largely through the mediumship of her counsellor, Mrs. E., a well-known healer and speaker. This lady trained her in all things, and did not appear to like or approve of me at all.

Relationships were not helped with either Mother or Patrick, by my desire to have a second child. From the time my active son was thirteen months old, I had known another soul drew near and waited a body to inhabit. This child, like my son, belonged to my destiny, and I had no wish at all to avert it. Yet I also understood quite practically why those closest to me were so against another baby. I had my hands more than full already with a determined young man who had screamed perpetually with rage and frustration throughout his brief existence — because he could not crawl when it was time to sit, or walk when it was time to crawl, or build bricks when time to walk, or draw as soon as his plump little hands could hold a crayon.

For nearly a year I pleaded with Patrick, who pointed out repeatedly all our obvious lacks — a home of our own not being the least of them. But of his own accord he capitulated when a rented cottage seemed about to be offered us. This hopeful prospect was promptly thwarted by events outside our control, but destiny cannot so easily be sidetracked, and my daughter was born prematurely in a blizzard one raging morning in early February.

This pregnancy had been dismal; different in every respect from the one preceding. Patrick was morose and Mother increasingly hostile, so there was no husbandly comfort, and no motherly commiseration. One bitterly cold January morning she had told me sharply to find other accommodation, and I had spent the ensuing hour overwhelmed with hopeless tears. The baby was breech, which did not help matters, and laid on a vein that varicosed painfully. Eventually the child turned, but not correctly, and my untimely labour was overlong and agonising, unaided by drugs for the baby's sake. At some point during the last exhausting hours I became aware of hovering above my body, and the nucleus that was 'I', registered dispassionately that if the pain did not soon cease I would be unable to enter it again. Seemingly at once, a nurse entered and gave me a minimal shot of pethidene.

My daughter came into the world in silence, and after a few anxious moments began mercifully to cry — a thin, high wail quite unlike the impassioned advent of her brother. I lay for what seemed eternity in the labour room, unable to be moved, drifting along grey tunnels towards a door and consistently turned back. I was given a blood transfusion, though not enough it seemed, and soon the troublesome vein thrombosed, creating further problems. Undoubtedly for some hours I was "very poorly" as the hospital said.

But my daughter was sweet, and thereafter proved my joy and consolation. She was a plump little baby, as pretty as she was good. She had my mother's delicate bones and aristocratic features, which at once endeared her to her grandparents, and was so angelically feminine her father was captivated on sight. She did great credit to the pink frills and lace trimmed bonnets, and evoked continual admiration from all and sundry. Her brother, who exhibited no signs of personal jealousy, now or ever, responded instead by obvious symptoms of feelings of inadequacy — though through no lack of attention on my part, for I could not have loved him more.

Yet it was still a long way from being 'roses'. When Teresa was three weeks old, Mother told me some cutting 'home-truths' about myself, derived from her recent session with Mrs. E. I was as yet pathetically weak, and had already outraged my husband by my shamefully incomplete recovery (he had stayed from work two days with me, and that should be enough!). I stood on the landing with the baby in my arms as Mother continued down the stairs, still speaking heedlessly of how she had put me upon a pedestal when a girl, and now I had fallen down and would never be restored — for any good qualities within me she had given me herself.

In my tired brain something stirred in mute and inarticulate protest, and for a ghastly moment came the impulse to throw my adored baby over the bannister. Sick and trembling I ran into our sittingroom, holding her close, tears streaming unchecked. My son was for a short while with his grandfather in the workshops, and by the time he was returned to me I had pulled myself together. It would have been useless to protest of these things to my father, for he idolised Mother. Nor would he had understood the mechanics of spiritualism on which she set such store. But the bouts of faintness, palpitation and anguished fear that came after that day, took months to overcome, and had to be grappled with alone. I grew up a little more, and found the beginnings of inner strength; but not without much suffering.

Now began a purposeful series of events which brought me to a state of spiritual preparedness — the necessary requisite for what lay ahead. Before embarking on this, I must say that from hereon, although it wasn't by any means 'roses', neither was it all gloom either. There were redeeming moments, and I had good relationships with other young mothers who met on the recreation ground, or at the clinic, or in each other's houses (those that had such blessings) most afternoons. Sometimes my mother was her old, friendly self, proud of her lovely grandchildren, gracious and charming. Sometimes too, Patrick was goodtempered, witty and humorous. Also, despite his alcoholic proclivities and quite marked good looks, he was faithful, and took no interest in other women. He was also hardworking, and highly skilled as a tradesman. He and my father were not really compatible by temperament, but Father respected his working ability and abundant stamina. He and my mother, however, maintained a wary truce, each recognising in the other a powerful potential adversary. One of my biggest problems was that in trying to please one, I invariably offended another, and could not hope to conciliate them all at the same time.

After five months of struggle with faintness and ill-health, my mother at last seemed to grasp I was not recovering properly from my confinement. One evening I had felt so weak and unwell, I was hardly able to get down the stairs to answer the door and then to speak sensibly to the man who stood there. Everyone else was out, and I prayed continually not to 'blank out' and leave my infants unattended. Mother was first to return, and feeling really frightened I broke down, unable to continue alone any longer. She was suddenly kind, and the next day arranged for me to attend Mrs. E.'s for healing whilst she sat-in with the children.

Whether it was this that helped me, or her unexpected gesture of affection, or the course of iron tablets she bought me, I could not say; perhaps some element of each, for my overstrung system began slowly to relax, and the faintness recede. But contact with Mrs. E. was a mixed blessing. She wasn't interested in my psychism, or in me; and unlike Mother and her other clients, I had no money to place in the pretty china dish in her hall — my mother kindly paid for my appointments.

Several times I attended 'circles' in which Mrs. E. gave clairvoyance — I regret I cannot recall now any of the messages received, but apparently the vibrations "dropped" as I entered the room, so Mother reported, making the atmosphere less satisfactory for everyone else, and Mrs. E. informed her I was "materialistic" like my father, and not spiritually orientated like herself. My stock again went down, and as my health improved, my visits ceased.

One incident I will mention for the benefit of those who incline to the view that mediumship must go hand in hand with saintliness. I sent Mrs. E. a gift of boxed soaps that Christmas as a gesture of thanks — the nicest I could afford — and learned later from a lady whose integrity, if not her discernment, is beyond reproach — that Mrs. E. unwrapped my gift in her presence and "slung it from one end of the room to the other", declaring it "cheap, like the sender".

My reputation for materialism had derived from the previous year, and was actually the forerunner of the preparatory events referred to. In the local paper one evening I had noticed an advertisement detailing a pair of investment cottages for sale. They were located further along the road in which we lived, and seemed remarkably inexpensive at £550, even as an investment.

I had for many months followed house prices with interest whilst haunting the offices of estate agents for possible rentals. On Patrick's wage we had been unable to save the necessary deposit to purchase even the smallest house — at least, not without him foregoing his personal expenditure on beer and cigarettes, which he was unwilling to do; but it occurred to me suddenly that some possibility lay here, in the cottages — which I promptly inspected, knowing at once they were a bargain.

The following day I contacted the agent who said he could raise 80—90% on them at the low figure asked; then with palpitating heart I approached my father and suggested he put down the deposit and we have one each — he could have the better, corner cottage, and Patrick would pay the mortgage for both. Prices were rising and we could resell them shortly for a much higher sum. Father was non-committal but went to look, and said immediately he would buy them outright and we could arrange to repay him for 'ours'. Only then was I brave enough to tell Patrick of this 'fait accompli', not having found the courage to broach it before — and he greeted it with native caution.

My father was a builder but had not previously bought old property as an investment. Having given his assistance, he left it to me to arrange resale, and was very pleasantly surprised when both cottages sold almost at once to separate purchasers at a most substantial profit. As the project was in his name, there having been no time for mortgage-raising, he received the completion cheques and remade the excess on ours out to Patrick alone, not even for us jointly, and Patrick opened a personal bank account with it.

We had enough now for a deposit on a small house, but to my distress he was reluctant to make the commitment — thinking of eventually buying land and becoming a self-employed builder. I, of course, was frantic for somewhere *now* and fumed with frustration... but I could not touch the money nor do anything about it.

To cap matters my parents made plain (through my mother) how very fortunate we were to receive money in this fashion, as if they had made us a gift. Perhaps they considered they had, as they need not have handed it over. I was naturally *very* grateful, but it upset me that the fact of their own windfall was ignored, for it would not have come about without my initiative; and the entire episode left me feeling most uncomfortable and mercenary.

Curiously enough my father supported Patrick's decision to delay house-purchase in favour of land, and my desperation grew. My efforts at persuasion had no effect save a futile compromise, for Patrick agreed to buy a caravan, though not the size requested — this one was 14′ x 7′ — and it was placed at the bottom of the garden and roughly fenced for David's benefit. I was pregnant at the time, and the benefit was far outweighed by other factors. The nights were bitterly cold, and the small stove filled our minute abode with fumes and draughts. All water had to be fetched from a stand-pipe on the house itself, and after several weeks of absolute misery I could take no more, and insisted we move back to our former rooms to sleep and to cope with washing etc. — hence my mother's annoyance that bleak January morning. Eventually the hated caravan was sold, but we still lived in 'rooms'.

In the October following Teresa's birth, I dreamt we moved into a small house which looked just like those further along the street — flat-fronted and without a hall. As we moved in, a funeral procession left the house next door. I wondered if the dream was symbolic, as we had less than a year now to wait for a council house, six years being the current waiting time.

Some weeks later, however, I again took note of a newspaper advertisement, with the same inner sense as before of its personal significance. It concerned a small house in Bermuda Terrace for which the owner asked £1,250, or near offer, and gave a telephone number. I phoned him, and asked if he would grant a second mortgage for any deficit between valuation and the amount we had available, providing we paid him the full asking price. He thought it over and said yes, and I at once placed both children in the pram and hurried along to look at the house. It was identical to those further along the street in which we lived — hall-less and flat fronted. There was also no bathroom, but the structure had been well-maintained and was sound.

Fearfully I told Patrick, and urged him to look too. He did, though unwillingly, but was unsure what to do and consulted my father. Both thought it too dear — neither being familiar with the market value of old property, unlike myself, who knew it was not dear at all. Eventually they compromised. Father offered to loan the deposit if we "beat down" the price, and we could then use our own capital for modernisation. The rear garden backed onto a narrow road, and was thus ideally suitable for use as a builder's yard if Patrick some day set up on his own; and this was the deciding factor. With trepidation I bartered the price until Father was satisfied, and a fortnight before Christmas we moved in. I could hardly believe it — at last my own home, and a garden for David, who was now three and a half. Teresa was ten months old and crawling busily into everything. The move was complex, as anyone coping with the very young will appreciate, but the results were rewarding.

Early in January, the old gentleman next door passed away, and a procession did leave, just as I had seen in my dream. I pondered on this repeatedly.

We lived in Bermuda Terrace for two and a half years and it proved itself a fruitful testing ground in many ways. Money, or rather the lack of it, was a perpetual nightmare and I racked my brains each week to make it go round. Patrick was moody and increasingly resented working for my father at an hourly rate, observing the excellent profits made from his able foremanship. Nightly he went out to cheer himself up, and nightly I stayed at home with the children. But I read, needleworked, and occupied myself with domestic tasks, and though often lonely I was seldom bored for there was always plenty to be done. Yet solitude and quietness had their compensations, and the many prayers I offered up to keep at bay the feelings of faintness that still dogged me daily at odd times, yielded a deepening perception of the normally unseen.

I often became aware of a gentle Presence watching over me, and one night I saw clearly a beautiful nun in a pale blue robe, holding a lighted candle towards me. She shielded the flame with her hand, and I knew the light was to show me the way. Another symbol she indicated was a magnolia tree in bud — which represented the aspirational aspect of myself, and suggested the possibility of a later flowering.

On a less personal level, once when I sat with my children on my lap, having listened to a story for the under-fives on the radio — the soft strains of 'Roses of Picardy' from the 1914 war engrossed my previously wandering attention. Suddenly the room changed, and for a timeless moment appeared much as it had done when we bought it, but the old range was lit (there was now a modern stove) and many pictures covered the walls. Framed in the doorway stood a little old lady listening to the music, her face sad and wistful. I later described her to our next-door neighbour, who said with amazement I had given an accurate description of the last tenant but one, down to her knotted, rheumaticky hands. This could have been a time-slip, or an apparition, but I think it more likely that the latent emotion within myself evoked by the song — reminiscent of so many young men who died tragically — enabled me to translate visually the imprint of some long-past incident similarly charged; like re-projecting a fragment of film on a screen.

With spring came epidemics, and David lay for four days with a raging, undiagnosed fever which could have been polio, but was eventually deemed a virus. It alarmed me dreadfully and proved an ominous herald. In September he started school, and was never there for more than a week without acquiring a cold, cough, chill or worse. That first abysmal winter he had influenza three times in various forms, a severe bout of whooping-cough, and glandular fever. The whooping-cough brought him to a shadow of his former sturdy self and kept him three months from school, by the end of which time he was spitting blood. Mrs. E. terrified me by warning me by telephone that he could be tubercular. Coming from her, a professional medium, my fears can be imagined; but X-rays revealed the trouble as collapsed capillaries, which quickly healed, and I was deeply thankful for this mercy.

Whatever David brought home, the baby Teresa developed in lesser measure, save for measles which she managed to have worse, and in our second summer she too, came close to death. But they were robust children, and with love and care recovered well. I also had my own share of illness, perhaps because I was still low from Teresa's birth; and for two years I was repeatedly unwell much to Patrick's exasperation. My mother put it all down to nerves which was most unfair — but at least ensured that it need not be taken seriously, and I coped as best I could. Even when commanded to bed by the doctor, replete with penicillin for a septic throat, and both children bouncing cheerfully beside me — the myth of self-made illness did not die. Only Patrick could be ill without this stigma, and when he was, the house was plunged in gloom, for there was no pay without work when on hourly rates in those days, even if one worked for one's father-in-law, and his frustration and resentment was like a fog descending on us all.

Before Christmas I had produced two shattering attacks of pain in my chest after struggling with heavy loads, and our kindly doctor asserted I needed more rest. This however, was quite out of the question, and neither Mother nor Patrick appeared to hear when I mentioned it. Now, of course, I understand how things seemed from their point of view, and how very inconvenient my illnesses must have been, but at the time I could only see my own need, the neglect of which pierced me as a betrayal of love. I plodded on day by day praying beseechingly that I should be spared to care for my children, and mercifully the heart pains did not recur.

In our second spring at Bermuda Terrace, Patrick decided to leave my father's employ and obtained the offer of a responsible position with a large building firm. On acquainting Father with this fact (much to parental consternation) he was immediately forestalled by the offer of a share of the profits on the new project now under way at Teversham, providing he would stay on. My brother was promoted at the same time — the opportunity both had long awaited, and Patrick shrewdly weighed his possibilities and remained. He worked like a beaver, all hours, every day including Sundays, and I hardly saw him at all; for when he left work he changed clothes, ate, and went to his pub. This became our pattern of life for many years, and though I accepted it in good spirit, (having little choice about it) of necessity it threw me back onto my own resources, and proved the perennial impetus for my inward turning aspiration.

By late autumn, with his share of the promised profits Patrick had purchased a surplus plot of land at Histon from my father, of irregular shape, and used formerly as a rubbish dump. It fringed the small, select development still under construction, and he at this point finally left my father's business and set up on his own, though he continued to sub-contract Father's brickwork. I was pleased about this from the business angle and gave him every support and encouragement; but the Histon plot, purchased solely for its cheapness, gave me a feeling of apprehension, I was not sure why. I simply could not accept my perception that one day I would be obliged to live there, and firmly squashed any intimation that dared to infiltrate my errant faculties.

I grew desperately lonely. The days were busy enough, and most afternoons enriched by the company of other young matrons, but the sole contents of our conversations were children and domestic affairs, and I yearned longingly for something more. On a swift whim one evening I took David's water-paints and roughed out spring flowers from memory. The result pleased me, and I began to paint each evening when Patrick had gone out and the children were asleep. These efforts were always of flowers — their imaged loveliness pressing to the forefront of my mind from long suppressed creative impulses which now sought release.

My brother was surprised by my ability and encouraged me with a gift of oils for Christmas, which really gladdened my heart. The colours mixed from the oils affected me — I indrew deeply some reverberating essence from their vibrant hues, absorbing warmth from flame, rose, orange, crimson and sunshine yellow that fed the starved emotions within me, and awoke again that stratum of myself that found joy in artistic expression. Patrick, unfortunately, did not like to arrive home and find me surrounded by paper and paint. He admired what I did, but it was casually expressed, and he soon made it clear that enough was enough. A wife who painted was an alien commodity, and this tendency, like dancing, poetry, authorship and clairvoyance, was not to be encouraged. So I continued only when quite sure I would be undiscovered, to eliminate the otherwise inevitable disruption; and buried my hurt and resentment, as my mother before me, beneath duty and love.

It is strange to recall that whatever inconsideration was meted out to me, it never affected my power to love, which seemed to spring from some sterling and indestructible inner source. With Patrick in particular, all affection could easily have faded away, as he held my daily wellbeing literally in his hand. He was, as already mentioned, in those days exceedingly handsome, and even my mother said he could "charm a bird off a tree" when he chose — but he did not philander, and when in the right frame of mind was a warm and affectionate person, which made up for much. Yet when really upset I lost sight of this, and would oblige myself to remember his unhappy childhood, and the lost scholastic opportunities he felt so keenly — he frequently worked on the roofs and in the courts of Trinity, and smouldered quietly but violently at the sight of young men in gowns to whom he should have been a compatriot by right of intellect, instead of the nondescript workman in overalls they brushed past unheedingly.

And if these reflections did not melt the built-up shell of hurt around me, I thought of the boy of nineteen in India, following-up the army through the battlefields of Imphal with all their horrors — and of the Burma jungle still spiked with guerillas, and a frightened young wireless operator enduring amoebic dysentery, malaria, conjunctivitis and foot-rot. Invariably it worked like a charm.

In early January I had a sudden, strong premonition one morning that something unusually unpleasant was about to occur, and a day or two later the scaffolding on which Patrick had been working (not erected by himself) collapsed and threw him fifteen feet to the ground. By a miracle he escaped serious injury, though he cracked two ribs, fractured a leg, jolted his spine, cut his head, and suffered extensive bruising. The pain and shock were formidable, and for hours he lay shaking violently, holding my hand.

Things had been increasingly strained for many months between us, and this sharp reminder of how easily we could be torn asunder, brought us closer and healed a widening breach. Difficult and badtempered though Patrick undoubtedly was, he had indomitable courage. For seven weeks he hobbled painfully with a stick, and could have stayed home for seven more, but he flung it aside, defied doctor's orders, and went back to work.

Already plans had been drawn up by myself, submitted and passed, for a bungalow on the Histon plot, and he forced himself now to dig footings in the rock hard, still-frozen soil of early March. Ignoring pain in back and leg alike he worked like a madman, and the genial labourer who worked with him grew quite concerned — but he heeded no-one, neither doctor nor wife, and kept up this frenzied pace for years, acquiring the reputation of a slave-driver. Nobody worked with him for long, save the Irish, who could work as hard as they drank. It paid off, of course, financially; but apart from his personal pocket money, all proceeds of this industriousness were ploughed back, and somewhat ruefully I accepted that any accrued benefits would have to be waited for, for apart from new curtains when next we moved, they certainly did not come my way then.

There were other problems now to fill my mind. With brighter weather David played outside, and managed consistently to evade my vigilance by climbing up to unbolt the high gate and play out in the rear street with other children. This street had been a quiet backwater when we bought the house, but owing to prolonged, extensive roadwork on the almost adjacent main road, most transport now took a short cut from one route to the next via this narrow lane, and heavy lorries bore down at reckless speed to the terror of other young mothers and myself. The pavements were thin, uneven strips, and my heart was in my mouth each time I stormed out and brought my enraged son back in, where he could have as many children as he liked — but naturally they did not wish to stay in the garden with him, it was more exciting in the street.

I produced a fear dream in which a lorry thundered by as my small son stepped off the pavement — terrified, I ran, but the road was clear and there had not been an accident. I felt though, that the dream held a warning.

Some children, sad to say, were less strictly supervised than mine, and an accident involving the loss of sight in a four year old's eye, caused added alarm. A child had aimed an arrow in the street referred to, and there was pandemonium. I began searching for another place to live, and plagued Patrick, whose mind was on other things, to sell our house and buy one in an area safer for the young.

In April, after much persuasion, he agreed to purchase a house near our former home in Richmond Road, with a small but pretty garden, well fenced and hedged, and ideal for Teresa who had now turned three. It was much larger than our present abode and in excellent condition; I contemplated taking a lady lodger to increase my housekeeping money, who might also sit in for me occasionally and enable me to attend the odd lecture. I began to feel unusually hopeful and happy.

One night I dreamed very vividly and disturbingly. I sat in the white walled, sunny area at the back of the proposed house, surrounded by all the things I had loved from my childhood days. I felt relaxed and contented — then suddenly became aware of a Presence — He of the white robe, and a firm voice which said, clearly and strongly *yet without sound* — "Cherish not the illusion, but seek the Reality". And rapidly, one by one, all my possessions faded from sight, the lovely house disappeared, and I was completely alone.

A few days later the owner of the house telephoned to say he had received a further offer, and did we wish to increase ours? The sum involved was fifty pounds, and meant we would have to find another one hundred — but our house had found an immediate buyer at £1,550 and I was sure it would be alright. Patrick, when informed of this, did not unfortunately believe the vendor, and refused point-blank. He said he had been having second thoughts anyway — the house was old and he already thought it too dear. Our own contract was signed and we were committed beyond recall; he would cancel his bungalow sale and we would have to go there.

I locked myself in the bathroom and cried. Having been subconsciously afraid all along that I should be forced out to Histon, my worst fears seemed realised.

But there was a reprieve. Some weeks beforehand I had noted a double plot of land for sale quite near my father's home, and pointed it out to Patrick, who would soon need further work. He said two plots were out of the question — he could only raise enough capital for one, and the plot was narrow and could not be split — the houses would have to be semi-detached. This of course I knew, yet my mind held to it like a limpet. Good building land was scarce, and I was reluctant to let pass what I knew to be a productive opportunity. I contacted the agent concerned and suggested we pay for one plot outright, and the second from the proceeds of the first house sold. If he could arrange this, we would guarantee him sole selling agency of both. And he did arrange it. Blandly and swiftly, to Patrick's astonishment. The confirmation came immediately after my disappointment over the house. Patrick then mentioned both matters to my father while working on his site.

Father had not known this particular land was for sale and said at once he would purchase the whole, and Patrick and he could have one plot each — his own architect could design the semi's, and Patrick could contract the brickwork for both. Furthermore, it was a shame to forego his bungalow sale, which was a profitable one — why not keep all his assets, and move into the semi when built? In the meantime he suggested we return to our former rooms for several months — the children, after all, were older now...

Amazingly, Patrick considered this — then, even more surprisingly agreed. Speculative building was a hair-raising business without adequate capital, and bank loans had already cut into his profits. It was a big temptation, and he closed his eyes to possible problems.

Bewildered and uncertain though I was, I clutched at the proposal as an escape from the isolation and loss of friendship that Histon represented to me, and for a few weeks all went well. Father purchased the land, thus negating my proposition, and the plans were immediately prepared by his architect.

In the middle of May Patrick suddenly became ill — so seriously I called the doctor in alarm. He had a huge quinsy which had virtually blocked his throat, and sent his temperature soaring. The doctor gave him a massive dose of penicillin (to which he was unfortunately allergic) and said there was no recourse but to remove his tonsils. This was speedily arranged for four weeks time.

Poor Patrick went back to his site as soon as he was well enough. The bungalow was almost finished now, and the prospective owner anxious to exchange contracts. In a fortnight we were due to leave Bermuda Terrace and return to my parents house. I told myself it would not be so bad — David was at school, and Teresa was a happy, good-tempered child. I could keep them out of doors through the warm summer months, and before winter came we would be in our own new home.

But Father (or Mother) had perhaps had second thoughts about living with their grandchildren, for he suggested quite casually to Patrick that we should live in the two main workshops instead — Patrick could re-emulsion them. This, too, was meekly accepted. Unfortunately, apart from being very cobwebby and draughty, the workshops also contained the workmens toilet — in the innermost room at that, and Patrick assumed it would now be out of bounds and some other arrangement made. I doubted this, and pressed him uneasily to make sure. He was annoyed by my persistence yet sought out my father nevertheless, and learned that, regretfully, it would have to remain in their use...

He came straight home from this conversation in a state bordering on apoplexy, so great was his rage. Swearing violently and prolifically about my father, he cancelled his bungalow sale within the hour. There was no doubt at all now that we should have to go to Histon. I produced a searing attack of migraine and then resigned myself to the inevitable, and Patrick a few days later went fuming miserably into hospital with the bungalow still unfinished, and our removal plans haywire. But it wasn't his fault, and I collected my wits together and did what was necessary. Much as I disliked the thought of Histon, the challenge of restoring order from chaos was stimulating, and I worked with a will.

My father kept the land. The architect-designed semi, when costed, turned out to be too dear for us, as it incorporated a number of expensive features my own designs lacked, and Patrick refused to buy it. In a half-hearted effort at compensation, Father offered him, for purchase, a building plot on the other side of the town, acquired from the brewery for whom he did contract work. It was in a no better area than Bermuda Terrace — in my view much worse, and I had no wish to live there. Moreover it was one plot, not two.

I felt quite cheated all round, and wished, not for the first time, that I too, was a man. If I had been, no-one could push me around in the way they did now. But I was simply a daughter, wife and mother; and my business capacities were utilised, but unacknowledged, either in words or cash.

Just before leaving Bermuda Terrace, I dreamed I was standing in Richmond Road beneath the old lilac tree that hung over a fence. It was in full bud and beginning to burst into bloom. My white robed Companion, deeply sensed and dimly seen, spoke very seriously to me. He said I could not have what I wanted just at this time, but there was a reason for this. Later, I could come back to the place of my childhood, not to the first house available, but to the second. Two numerals were held before my eyes — one was clearly a three, but the second was misty. I thought it was a three too, and recorded it when I awoke.

Mother loaned me two little books around now, lent by a friend, and I soaked up their contents like parched earth soaks rain. They were published by the Buddhist Society, and struck a deep chord in me. Some spiritualist literature also came my way, and though its appeal was not as great, it was nevertheless manna to my seeking soul. I thought about these things as I busied myself making curtains, and had the indefinable feeling that I should not always remain in the state of darkened consciousness I lived in now.

There was little time to dwell on it. Our imminent removal necessitated perpetual activity, and the children's presence required the immediate re-establishment of order at the other end in the unfinished bungalow. Set in its plot of waste land thick with nettles and building rubble, I found the prospect most unprepossessing; but by the time Patrick came out of hospital the rooms were arranged and had some semblance of homeliness. Feeling far from well, in his usual fashion he threw himself straight into work — hanging doors, slatting the airing cupboard, completing the bathroom, painting and emulsioning. Fortunately he soon regained strength, and turned then to his newest project on the brewery building plot — purchased as nothing else at this time was available. Once more I barely saw him, and the temporary closeness of his illness and our joint endeavours was gradually lost.

Both children developed chicken-pox as soon as we moved, and after recovery, David started his new school, and Teresa found her first friend — a charming little boy who lived opposite, and they rapidly became inseparable. The days suddenly stretched emptily before me. I missed my friends desperately, and the sociable afternoons, the familiar shops and acquaintances. I could not afford the fares to go often to see them, and anyway was bound by David's schooltimes.

My mother was very busy at this phase of her life and went daily to Mrs. E.'s as her foremost assistant. She allowed me to visit her every Tuesday morning, and this was the highlight of the week. Mrs. E. had pronounced that in all probability I should have to live in Histon for three years "for discipline", and that I should take up something useful like dressmaking (which I loathed). Mother's own feelings confirmed this, and I was panic-stricken. The bouts of faintness and palpitation returned with a vengeance, and in despair I saw a doctor, who prescribed pills for what he termed 'anxiety states' which nearly knocked me out with stupor, so I would not take them. I felt lonely, friendless, penniless and ill.

I tried hard to make the best of things. Seeking an outside interest and companionship, I asked if I might join the Women's Institute — Patrick agreed with reluctance, although it only meant he need stay in for one evening a week. I went twice, and was given a part in the drama-group play, but the third time he refused to remain in with the children, and I had to send away the embarrassed woman who called for me.

That was the end of my venture into night-life. I cried, of course, but it made no difference. Once more I turned to painting, producing, I felt, my best effort yet; but after the first two pictures the heart went out of me. It was all so solitary, so unshared — so pointless. My last attempt was stark and bleak and dead like myself. I had captured my state so well that to look at it was frightening — trees in leaf, sky, and a stream, but so still, so without life... so dull. As a last resort, I even begged Patrick to let me have another baby, but that, too, was denied. He did not want any more. I ought, it seemed, to be grateful beyond words to live in a brand new bungalow. I noted however, that he did not change his pub, and each evening he went back again to Cambridge.

I dreamed one night that I was taken again to Richmond Road, into the front bedroom of a house formerly occupied by an old gentleman who had recently died. My Companion gently informed me that soon I should come here to live. I was greatly agitated and cried "No, no, no — I mustn't come back — Mother says I must stay in Histon three years..." He smiled and shook his head. "You will come *here*", he said.

Shortly after we moved into the bungalow, a house had become vacant near my parents home, and on one of my Tuesday visits I inspected it. It stood large and detached in a beautiful garden, with a wide side access that would take another house. I did my utmost to persuade Patrick to buy it, but he would not even look at it, though it was for sale at a lower figure than the value of the bungalow, and included the land which no one had thought of submitting for planning permission. He therefore missed out on a sound proposition he could have had for the asking, and ironically it sold at an even lower figure soon afterwards. His mind was elsewhere, and all my pleas to sell the wretched bungalow fell on deaf ears.

I dug frantically in our rock-hard garden to pass the time, and made dresses, coats, bonnets and nightwear for Teresa until my arm ached from pushing the antiquated sewing machine, but nothing seemed to help me. I would work energetically for a while, then feel suddenly faint and have to stop, my heart racing and my legs trembling and weak. It alarmed me dreadfully; and worse still was the numbing of the mind that followed, and I would run my wrists under cold water in desperation to try to force myself back again to normal consciousness.

I became afraid of myself and of the impulse to violence the frustration within me forced to the surface. Having always been quietly behaved and, I believe, of a gentle nature — the things found inside me were foreign to all I had previously known and caused me untold bewilderment and distress. I prayed almost ceaselessly for strength.

Foolishly I tried to tell Mother how I felt, and her response was to sternly give me a little book on prayer, which I dutifully read. All my former attempts to pray had been spontaneous uprisings from my heart, asking help, or giving thanks — but I had never prayed in the traditional way. Now I really tried in earnest to talk to God as the Church instructed. It proved a sadly barren exercise. I tried to locate Him deep within me, but my mind was empty, and I was empty too.

I discovered I was nothing. This awareness was so real that it was horrifying. What was I? Where was I? Where was God? I stilled myself, then recoiled in despair. 'I' did not seem to be anywhere. There was a hollow ring that was my body — and it was quite, quite empty. In my heart I might believe in God, but in my mind I was forced to conclude I did not. When confronted with the infinite, my mentality wavered, and fell away. It could not apprehend God of itself.

Living with the results of this distressing introspection was terribly nerve-racking; yet I knew even when at my lowest ebb that a little kindness and consideration — a glimmer of understanding, and a taste of freedom, would have healed my troubled psyche completely.

But however legitimately resentful of Patrick I felt at times, it was impossible to prolong it to any fruitful conclusion; for to express it even mildly caused havoc — black moods and ill-temper, and made life miserable for everyone without achieving what I most desired. I thus learned, through necessity, an inner discipline which schooled my urge for equality and my longing for affinity, into a silent acceptance of what I could not alter; and channelled my powerful aspirations into the darkness of my innermost source.

Late in November, Patrick suddenly asked me to put in a low offer for a small house he had noticed for sale in Richmond Road. It had previously been sold, or so he assumed, about eight months ago, but for some reason was now readvertised. On enquiry I found that the earlier sale had capsized through the discovery of extensive woodrot beneath the floorboards. This did not bother Patrick at all. The offer went in, and after some delay was accepted. He then asked me to visit the house and prepare plans for its total renovation, which I did, learning at the same time it had been the former home of the old gentleman mentioned in my dream. The number, incidentally, was thirty-three. When the plans were passed Patrick told me that *now* he was ready to place our bungalow for sale, and we would move in the springtime as soon as modernisation on the other was complete.

All the foregoing was by Patrick's instigation — it was one of the very few transactions not required of me to set into motion. His intention, naturally, was to provide work, then to resell as soon as a further proposition made it practicable — yet even so the information given me in sleep had proved entirely accurate. This uncanny sequence of events affected me profoundly, and drew my attention deeply inwards, seeking the source of the fore-knowledge given.

In January, Patrick and my father quarrelled. It was the first time their mutual antagonism had flared into words and occurred during a telephone conversation about sub-contract work. Father delivered the parting shot before banging down the receiver. The following morning, hard as granite, Patrick went into Cambridge to confront him with his accusations face to face. Acutely I sensed a disruptive consequence, and entreated him not to go, but he was adamant. I cried until my stomach retched, and could not stop till long after he disappeared down the road.

While I waited, wave upon wave of blackness seemed to roll over me and I felt that something momentous was about to happen in my life. Some two hours later he returned, his face like thunder, and so angry he could hardly speak. Despite my anxious protests he packed his case and left within the hour for Middlesbrough, his home town, refusing to wait and take myself and the children, who had been respectively at school, and a neighbour's, all morning. Withdrawn and aloof he went at once, and remained for five days, telephoning daily but refusing to return. Nor was there any certainty he ever would.

The countryside in January is not the best place to spend long nights alone when on the verge of a nervous breakdown. Sleep eluded me, and the relentless hours strained my endurance to its limit. It was at this juncture that I accepted that I was really alone in the world. My husband, love me though he may, could never see things from my angle, or consider *my* needs in times of stress. When confronted with personal problems himself, he invariably left me to my fate, and seemed not to understand the inner turmoil of the past four years.

I had loved him deeply, and the love remained; but for the first time I faced that for me it was not enough. I longed for something deeper, more inclusive and absorbing — an intangible something that could encompass and include my outer life and also the spiritual yearning in my heart. I let in the realisation that I could never fully depend on Patrick — that in extremity he could turn away from me; and at last confronted the fact that my marriage was not, *and could never be*, that union of essence which is the all in all of a true relationship, and had been my dream from my earliest recollection. And having accepted the incompleteness of my situation, and acknowledged painfully my aloneness... very gradually, from that day forward, I began to return to health.

After five days Patrick returned, and picked up the pieces of our life as if his exit from it had never been. He avoided my father for a while, but work outstanding inevitably brought them together. This was made easier by the fact that my father was chastened, as he realised his daughter and grandchildren had borne the brunt of his arrogant words. To his credit he put himself out to make amends, and afterwards handled Patrick with caution.

At the end of March I had an unusually vivid dream experience with a similar impact to that of twelve years ago — when first I had registered the cosmic Being who directed my inner development. In this experience (for it was not an ordinary dream) I stood in a circle of about twelve people, in a grassy place. It was drizzling slightly, and I waited in silence at my mother's side, feeling very young and immature. In the centre of the circle stood a shadowy Being, whom I knew to be our Teacher. The gathering was for a specific purpose — some sort of office was to be presented to one of our number, and I assumed this to be my mother. The symbol of office was a sword, invisible to all save the one who had power to hold it, and I saw my mother reach out her hand to receive it.

She must have taken it into her palm, for a mighty voice rang out, saying, "Give the sword to your daughter!" — she looked bewildered, and the voice cried out again, repeating its request. I heard her say "but I thought *I* was to lead..." and she made a movement with her hand, as if something was taken from it. Then the Being moved towards me, and told me to *prepare* to receive the sword. I was greatly afraid. His outline was just discernable, but my eyes could detect no trace of the weapon he held. I knew, however, that it was large and had a razor-sharp double blade, also that he or she who held it must run their fingers along its length, that others might know where it lay.

I stood dumbly, unsure and fearful, and felt the cold hardness of silver placed in my palm, and the weight of the sword as I gripped it to balance it upright before me. "Run your fingers along the blade," commanded the Being, his voice firm but gentle — "Don't be afraid!" Slowly and cautiously I did as I was bidden, and felt the knife-edge skim my skin. As inch by inch my fingers crept up the sword, my terror began slowly to dissolve, and gradually and luminously it began to shine, and faintly and dimly I found I could see it. When my fingers had reached two-thirds of the way up, the sword suddenly flamed into brilliance, its light and beauty both dazzling and unbelievable. A tremendous joy shook my heart — I lifted my face to the heavens, now pouring with rain which I felt on my cheeks, and cried out, over and over again, "I can see!... I can see!... I can see!" — then I awoke, tears streaming down my face, the overwhelming joy and gladness still pervading me.

I had no understanding of the dream, or what it meant in terms of the future. No inkling that in a sense it encapsulated my life. I was just an ordinary young housewife, heavily bound by the chains of matrimony and motherhood. Surrounded by materialistic people, my sole contact with those of similar interests was my mother, and my dreams and intuitions were the only things that set me apart from my kind. Yet they signalled something profound which my mind could barely grasp at, and indicated a pattern I was as yet too immature spiritually to perceive.

We left Histon just as spring broke in all its glory. The lilac bloomed early, and I remembered the promise made under the lilac tree. In April I walked happily along the loved and familiar roads, unaware their enchantment was broken. I was glad to be back in the city, but from then on I was rootless.

He knows the touch
of an ant's foot
moving in darkness
over a rock.
He always knows
what is in men's minds:
you would do well
to reflect on this.

Hakim Sanai, 'The Walled Garden of Truth'
translated by David Pendlebury,
Octagon Press Ltd. 1974 p. 24.

Hardly had we moved into the Cambridge house, when a powerful precognition infiltrated my consciousness. Its initial impetus was conveyed to me in a dream in which I stood at a bus stop in the city centre, and was approached by a middle-aged woman who placed a pellet of bread in my hand. Simultaneously, the voice of the Teacher said quietly, on an inner vibration, that here was something of great importance to me. I then found myself standing in the doorway of a house, from where I could see several wedding groups, one after the other, assemble further along the street, and at one point, a funeral. It was curiously reminiscent of Victoria Road, an area I much disliked. I next was upraised, as if by unseen arms, high into the air — so that I looked down on the road from a great height and could see surrounding landmarks clearly from the wider viewpoint above. We travelled fast along its length, and came soon to a forked turn, where a narrow lane led off from the main route. With a faint sense of apprehension I looked out on a rural scene, and was told that we must take this by-road, and not continue along the highway.

At the end of the dream, as I began to waken, I again heard the voice, externally now, vibrating soundlessly against my ear; it said, "Soon you will come to the little Red Gulch, where things will be much easier for you, and more as you want them." Then I was plunged, breathless and gasping, down a 'chute' and into my physical body.

I pondered the dream, which held both perturbation and promise, knowing beyond any possible doubt that I had seen symbolically what must inevitably occur. The words 'Red Gulch' seemed feasibly a projection of Rose Ford, and could refer to Roseford Road. Many times when David was a baby I had walked over the new and growing Arbury Estate, and each time I came to the junction of Roseford Road and the rough grassland scheduled for future building, my spirit had quickened, and I was filled with a deep, restless and unfathomable longing.

Perhaps the most important aspect of my dream was that I actually registered, in the process of waking, the mechanics of receptivity. This had not happened previously with such clarity. It revealed the brain as a finely tuned instrument which could adjust to the impress of other-dimensional experiences. There was an intermediary bridging mechanism, of subtle construction, which I termed a 'chute' for want of a better word, linking a finer level of existence with this one. If the linkage was sufficiently strong, and the brain adequately attuned, the life of the spirit could reflect itself via this channel or media, into the brain, and thus the body consciousness.

Throughout May I was unwell with what the doctor vaguely termed a germ in the kidney; but I had begun to note that I became ill after any particularly potent illumination, as if its registration involved some effort of adjustment or assimilation by the physical organism. At different times, throat, heart, kidneys and head were affected — though knowing the origin of the disturbance did nothing to alleviate it, unfortunately.

In less than a fortnight after my dream, Mother had passed to me a book loaned by her friend, Mrs. C. It was on the subject of Yogi Philosophy, and I read it through with growing wonderment. Page after page 'spoke' to me in the language of the heart. It was like re-entering a beloved country, long unseen and almost forgotten.

The book was my first introduction to such literature, and opened a new world to my questing soul which could be traversed even within the limits of my closed environment. When, months later, I eventually met Mrs. C., I felt with puzzlement that we had been in contact before, and it took several days for my fumbling brain to locate her; but she was unmistakably the woman of the dream, and the 'pellet of bread' was obviously a spiritual manna — the staff of life — which fed and enriched my searching mind. In the meantime other books, perhaps six in all, had followed the first, much to my gratitude and benefit.

Our brief stay in the Cambridge house was a great improvement on life in the bungalow. David had returned to his former school, Teresa played happily wherever I took her, and my days were pleasantly full and involved with women of my own age and situation. In the better climate that ensued between Patrick and myself, I found courage to try again for an occasional evening out, and tentatively suggested this. He seemed agreeable, and I planned to attend an advertised lecture one Thursday. About half an hour before starting out, he changed his mind, and went out himself even earlier than usual despite my anguished protests. It was a bitter pill, and took all my strength to fight down every element in myself that furiously rebelled at his selfishness, knowing if I voiced it there would be chaos and the rifts in our marriage would rapidly widen irreparably.

Why it had to endure I did not then know, but apart from the obvious problems of rearing children, I felt inside me I must make it work somehow. So I planted out a bed of seedlings in the front garden, swallowed my anger, and kissed him on his return. Looking back, I am amazed at my submission. I had a strong character, and my father's energy and initiative — yet I lived in virtual purdah. What Patrick deserved was smartly boxed ears and a few plates thrown at his head, plus uncooked meals, unwashed shirts, and a refusal of 'conjugal rights'. But such luxuries of emotional release were not permitted me, for the temper of the man I married would have blown a fuse — and I cared, idiot that I was, too much about him to chance it.

The Histon bungalow had sold quickly, and in June the cheque arrived. I thought at last a share of the profits would come my way, and I could buy books — but not so, they must all be ploughed back into the next project. As I did so much work of a varied nature to help — with an eye to the future I suggested we ought now to have a joint bank account, but this too was firmly vetoed, and Patrick told me if I didn't wish to help him, he would manage by himself.

I felt no defiance over this; no rage or bravado — simply defeat. That night I cried myself to sleep, imploring the white-robed Being to help me to understand *why* I must bear this lack of loving, in all who were close to me, save my young children.

My father was building now at Swavesey, twelve miles out from Cambridge, and offered Patrick a plot there. I urged him very strongly not to take it, and for once he was hesitant as he feared the distance might affect an eventual sale. Much work had been done on thirty-three which now had the appearance of a new house inside — the frontage had also been renewed with modern bay windows, and I knew Patrick was thinking of the profit he could reap if and when he sold it. In the meantime, having completed the brewery-land bungalow and found a possible purchaser, he sub-contracted for my father. In July we all succumbed to Asian 'flu; then Teresa caught whooping cough, though not too badly, and life moved on in its usual fashion.

Early in August an estate agent sent us a single, unsolicited leaflet advertising a house in Victoria Road for £1,550. It seemed uncommonly reasonable, so I made an appointment to see it. As mentioned before, I disliked the road intensely, but went because I was worried about David's pending change of school. He had turned seven and must move on next term to 'juniors' — the nearest being St. Luke's on Victoria Road — a mixed school which at present had a reputation for roughness. The thought of him crossing major roads without me amid the pushing throng of older boys made me feel sick, and I would have moved anywhere to ensure his safety.

The house was still occupied and was beautifully furnished, with an abundance of highly polished surfaces and velvety cushions. It looked gracious and inviting, and I suggested to Patrick that he ought perhaps to look at it. He did so, and was equally impressed, commencing purchase arrangements immediately and placing our own house for sale. It sold at once, and we prepared to move on after five months of residence.

A few nights before the vendors of our new abode moved out, I had a dismal dream of scouring a dirty house which looked almost as if it was falling to pieces. Feeling oddly disturbed, I went again to Victoria Road, and asked if I might take measurements for curtains. The owner had packed and was on the point of departure, and the house no longer had an air of comfort, but, curtainless and carpetless, revealed every formerly carefully concealed defect.

I said nothing to Patrick, as it was too late to alter things, but he looked at my face, and knew. That evening, having obtained the key, he entered the house in the dark, struck matches everywhere, and came away satisfied, saying he still thought we had a bargain. The next day he thought otherwise. We moved in, and Patrick promptly moved out, to the outside toilet, where he was very sick. Fear of making a bad speculation had always weighed heavily on him, and the bright morning sunlight was cruelly illuminating. I comforted him, feeling irrationally it could all be put right, encouraging him to relay our linoleum, then return to his own employment. I worked like a trojan in the meantime and probably broke all former records, for on David's return from school in the late afternoon the house was orderly, clean and comfortable, with rugs down, paintwork scoured and curtains hung — even chrysanthemums from the tiny garden adding their vibrant homeliness in a pot on the table, and the stacked unpacked boxes in the front sittingroom temporarily forgotten. Once more the ominous defects were obscured, and Patrick for a change was warmly and genuinely appreciative and said I had a "stout heart".

To reassure himself further he placed the house for sale again straight away, and having negotiated an immediate figure that was substantially more than we had paid, proceeded to cancel it, as we had nowhere to go; but his nervous system could now relax, and he went back to work in good spirits.

We had of course, only basics in the way of furniture — much of it passed on from my parents, and no great quantity of 'effects' — which explains in part the speedy nature of our rehabilitation each time we moved. Even in later years I always reckoned to have everything in order by the end of five days, though this naturally involved working non-stop till one dropped into bed, exhausted, late at night.

This particular house was quite near to St. Luke's Church and from its front door I saw several weddings as I came and went, and there were obviously funerals too, though these I did not pause to watch. It gave me a strange sense of astonishment when these events occurred, for it was like reliving the substance of a dream, and in the back of my mind I dwelt continually on the fact of foreknowledge and the counsel which accompanied it.

I have not attempted to include the many perceptions relating to side - issues — wishing merely to outline the main theme of a guided destiny — and would like to stress at this point that the marital disharmonies etc. sprinkled throughout the account were not inserted from self-pity, but to give background insight to a life which yielded extremely potent other- dimensional experiences. In tracing this route I have kept to how I *felt*, and was *affected* at the time, but much further on I saw the whole with different eyes, and the objective assessments made then create a more positive story. These, for obvious reasons, must be left out now.

We had lived in Victoria Road for six weeks when I felt I could no longer endure the uniform drab beige of the wallpapers with their faded patches and sundry marks. Patrick said we could not afford a decorator, so I insisted I could paper the walls myself. He doubted this, but stubbornly and greatly daring, I purchased materials against his account (and without his permission) embarking at once on the hall ceiling.

It was easier than I thought, and the wallpaper went on the walls with remarkable ease, transforming the drabness immediately. Not to be outdone, Patrick started on the sittingroom, and discovered among his other abilities that he was a competent decorator. Fired with enthusiasm by the joyful results, we worked our way diligently through the house. It took six weeks to complete, at the end of which I was exhausted; but the results were well worthwhile, and Patrick afterwards undertook all his own decorating instead of contracting it out, which made a considerable saving.

Having brought myself low I succumbed to a chill, followed by two sharp attacks of cystitis which unfortunately lowered my hard-won prestige. Teresa too, caused alarm by pitching over the headboard of her bed whilst it was moved out to paper the wall, and mildly concussing herself. A little later her closest friend developed polio, and we had a nightmare time at the end of the quarantine period when she produced stiffness and high fever, diagnosed eventually as tonsillitis. Her friend, fortunately, recovered well, but several local children suffered lasting disability, and there was a general air of worry and apprehension.

These trials took their toll and I felt increasingly depleted and unwell. One night, just before sleeping, I saw clairvoyantly a bright star overhead, like a herald, and a benign, austere figure robed in blue watching it steadfastly. Several nights later he appeared again, this time with a thorn-staff twined with briar roses, which I felt was proffered for my support. He looked directly at me, and simultaneously I understood I was to think of him as Father Joseph. This seemed rather odd, as I 'saw' him within my own head, projected as if on a screen behind my eyes — yet we appeared for a moment to be face to face, his eyes observing me intently.

I sensed him often after this, like an unseen but almost tangible presence; and he was indeed a staff on which to lean, for his sympathetic kindness reached me effectively whenever most needed. I felt he acted as an intermediary between myself and the white-robed Being, whose mode of manifestation was quite different and seemingly from a much finer dimension, one less concerned with the purely human emotions with which I grappled daily.

I dreamt too, and registered uneasily that one dream in particular was precognitive. In it I looked at the plain facade of a terraced house and was told I would live there. Its interior was crammed with heavy furniture and there was an atmosphere of gloom. A ground floor room had part-drawn curtains and contained a wheelchair and a wardrobe full of female clothing. Shoes were scattered over the floor, and a distraught man said he had kept it thus since his wife died, exactly as she had left it. The wheelchair was apparently hers. Through the window of the dim lit room I could see a pretty garden bright with sunshine. I then awoke.

Teresa was now at infant school and I had more time for my own affairs. I began to study in earnest, but soon found that certain books (their titles taken from the jacket covers of Mrs. C.'s) were unavailable at the library and would have to be purchased if I wished to read them. I did not know then of postal libraries attached to various organisations, and therefore asked Patrick if I could at last have a little money of my own to spend, as he now had the cheque for thirty-three, and also the brewery-land bungalow. He refused. We could not afford books, he said — he needed all we had for his newest project — he was thinking of buying the Swavesey land, as my father and brother had each sold a bungalow there without difficulty.

I felt dismayed about the land, and deeply certain that if he bought it he would regret it, but I could not help commenting that he could always find money for beer and cigarettes. This naturally caused extreme offence, and concluded any hopes I might have had.

By chance I learned later that he had loaned ten pounds to the man he employed as a casual labourer, and this really upset me. I smouldered inwardly over it for days, and realised at length that my resentment was in effect poisoning me. It grew so strong I could no longer deflect my thoughts, and found myself constantly in a state of hostility towards Patrick, unexpressed but ever present. My mother fed the flames on her weekly visit and called him, among other things, a man of straw — which was certainly untrue as he was anything but weak. I staunchly defended him as she was biased and merely depreciating my husband against her own — and I very well knew my father was little better. At last I grew scared at the strength of my errant emotion and one evening knelt on the floor at Patrick's side, begging him to help me, fearing if I continued like this I would cease entirely to love him. I told him I knew of his loan to L. and how this had affected me. He seemed suddenly to grasp that I was absolutely serious beneath my distress, and though very vexed, he was obviously shaken. Eventually he said he would give me £25, which he did the day following. I was able then to buy my books and other things long lacked, and the bitterness at once dissolved and we were friends again.

Patrick ignored my intuitions about Swavesey and bought a plot of land alongside my father's; but he also needed indoor work for the winter weather and I told him of a house now advertised in Histon Road and seemingly ripe for modernisation. At his request I inspected it, and knew it to be a sound speculation. When Patrick viewed it he agreed, but cautiously put in a lower offer than the figure asked, and it was turned down. I felt rather relieved over this, as the house had a plain frontage, was terraced, and fitted too well the details of my dream. It also stood on a busy main road no better than the one we lived on.

Shortly came another, more impactive dream relating to a different house entirely. In this I stood with Patrick in semi-darkness outside a double-bay-windowed dwelling in Richmond Road that adjoined, apparently, the home of my childhood's friend, Betty. Patrick looked thoughtfully up at the guttering and said he would buy it. In the shadows behind us, silent and watchful, was He of the white robe — and as I registered this I heard myself say, "You can't have this one, Patrick, it's already sold." A voice from the darkness remarked calmly, "Yes, it is sold, and will be sold again; but you will have it in the end." and I awoke feeling puzzled.

Several weeks passed, and out of the blue Patrick was recontacted by the agent handling the Histon Road sale, and told he could have the house at the figure he had offered as the other party had withdrawn; so it was purchased. There was, of course, no intention on his part of us living there — it was simply a job of work which was likely to prove quite profitable. He now had two projects soon well under way, and with frequent wet days, the work on the house proceeded rapidly and quickly outstripped the scheduled bungalow. Unfortunately though, it did not sell. Viewers were few and nobody seemed to want it. By late February Patrick was worried, for his capital was fast being absorbed and no purchasers were yet in sight for either venture. At length he did what later became a standard procedure — placed our house for sale as well, and if it sold first, we must live in the one remaining.

Ours sold immediately, probably because of its pretty decorations; and the new owner was in a hurry and wished us out fast. At this point we received an unexpected telephone call from another agent, who said the last of a group of new, semi-detached houses fronting Roseford Road was being drastically reduced to £2,150 to dispose of it quickly and get the builder out of difficulties. Would we be interested? He could raise us a 95% mortgage.

Interested! The world lit up again, and my grey forebodings about Histon Road dispersed like wraiths. To me it was the Mecca for which I was waiting, and joyously I informed my spouse, quite certain of his approval. But no, he would not as much as look at it. It was "too dear", he "didn't want such a large mortgage". His sights were fixed elsewhere, and my hopeful castle in the air tumbled to fragments.

The Histon Road project was finished as far as its new bathroom and kitchen were concerned, but still undecorated — and Patrick now suggested I help him do it, and if I did, he would give me a further fifty pounds from our present house sale as I had also done most of that. There was not really any choice. Our removal date was unalterable, and I had already shed the usual tears at having to go somewhere I did not want to.

Working alone in the house made me nervous, I could not say why, but it felt heavily oppressive. I also found it very tiring plodding backwards and forwards to the school to collect my children. Both came home for a meal midday as David had previously had his fill of school dinners, and I felt their close association with myself was beneficial to them in the midst of so much change. Halfway through the decorating I caught influenza, which was epidemic at that time — and Patrick sat on the side of the bed and swore at me when he realised I could not get out of it. It was unfair, he said. I did it on purpose. *He* had to keep going, why couldn't I? Poor, poor Patrick. I understood despite my misery. Life was hard and work-filled, and I was always being ill. Yet it hurt so much that he should slander me, and with such injustice — and I cried weakly and quietly until I lost myself in the lurid dreams of delirium.

We moved two weeks later, and I was very depressed. It was like entering bedlam. Our next-door neighbours played a radio loudly and constantly, all day and every day, and its din could not be avoided. As yet no fence had been erected in the rear, and their barking female dog attracted endless suitors who considered our garden commonland. I felt increasingly desperate to get out and away from the noise.

Another factor, far more serious, which I made no attempt to formulate to Patrick, was that the house was full of terrible words, and I soaked them up like a sponge. One by one they entered my thoughtstream as I worked in the empty sittingroom, the children at school and Patrick at Swavesey. Swear words and obscenities, clear and unmistakable, dropped into my mind. Not voices — there was nothing astral here, but words impressed on the atmosphere itself, and I could not shut them off. Terrified, I prayed constantly for help.

Our neighbour on the side opposite to the radio told me the recent history of the house; a man had lived there with his two children for a year after the lingering death of his wife, and would not change anything from the way it had been, nor dispose of her clothes. This naturally explained my dream. But there was another side to the story as I learned later when this neighbour, an elderly lady of the 'old school' knew me well enough to tell me. She informed me, with high colour and much shocked indignation, that the language heard through the wall during all-male games of poker, was "enough to turn your ears blue!"

A further revelation of the mind of the previous occupant came when I inadvertantly opened a letter addressed to him which looked like a circular. Inside was a brochure advertising most graphically the type of literature I did not then know existed. Even so, my supposed enlightenment was incomplete. Ignorant of the world's vices, I assumed that the format concerned male and female relationships, and that 'gay' meant vivacious; but the language was licentious, and I grasped I had simply absorbed someone else's very potent thought emanations. These, incidentally, subsided abruptly after the first three weeks, which was a mercy, as I might well have soon begun to doubt my own sanity.

During this time I had a disquieting dream in which we moved back again to 33, Richmond Road — but gone was the new plasterwork and white paint, and instead were walls grey with cobwebs, floorboards broken and rotted, and mice running out from the skirting. I concluded things had all been too much for me and that I was getting my wires crossed somewhere.

Frantically seeking escape from the fairground atmosphere adjoining my home, within a month of our move I had found a delightful Victorian property at the top end of Richmond Road, with five bedrooms plus outbuildings for the sum of £3,500 — a low figure even then. I pressed Patrick earnestly to buy it — I could cover the mortgage with ease by letting rooms, and the outbuildings alone, well-kept, and opening onto the prettiest garden, would make us charming living quarters. We could have entirely self-contained accommodation without any outgoings — and I fully expected him to be delighted. He went with me reluctantly to look. Yes, it was a very good idea. Yes, it could certainly be made to work. Yes, he thought I could do it on my own... but he still did not want the initial mortgage required to purchase.

Coming back along the street he stopped outside number 31, which had a newly erected 'For Sale' board in the front garden. "Now this is more what I want," he said, and asked me to enquire its price. I did so, my mind still fixed on No. 10, and the following day inspected it with him, and he put in an offer. It had a double-bayed front in quite good condition, but its floors were wood-rotted, there was no electricity or bathroom, and it needed complete modernisation throughout.

I had hopefully kept open the arrangement for the larger house, and the agent now sent us a letter pressing further action, but here Patrick dug in his heels and refused to comply. There was, as usual, nothing I could do about it, and I fumed silently at the loss of a golden opportunity. The offer for 31 was rejected, but some six weeks later the house was again for sale, and the situation repeated. Later still a letter arrived stating that the second purchaser had withdrawn and the offer could now be accepted; but Patrick was no longer sure that he wished to proceed — he had decided with great trepidation to buy a van on Hire Purchase, and this at present filled his horizon. Ever my own executioner I pointed out that the accepted figure was even less than he had given for 33, and this time there was no need to remove the frontage — it was therefore a watertight proposition; so he bought it. Thinking it over afterwards I realised it was next-door to the former home of another close friend of my childhood, Joyce — who was Betty's friend as well.

Like it or not, I had to adapt to a time in Histon Road, and realising this I stopped battling and tried to make the best of it. Patrick put up a fence, which at least freed us from the attention of dogs;

but the outlook was derelict and I commenced digging the narrow strip of earth near the side door and pressed in some plants to enliven the view. It was a drop in the ocean, for the garden was quite wide and unusually long, having marked affinities with a rubbish dump. Yet even to this one with time adjusted.

My daughter made friends with the little girl next door and I soon got to know our noisy neighbours, who were in fact warm and friendly people. Their house however was chaotic inside, as the poor mother was asthmatic and could do very little in the way of domestic work. They were not a fussy family anyway, and it upset me considerably to find my beautiful child on sunny Saturday mornings installed in a stuffy bedroom on the dusty floor, accompanied by a very unwashed dog, and eating buns kindly proferred from a kitchen swarming with flies. Having always been ultra-hygienic with my young to the point of idiocy, this caused me many apprehensions, all fortunately groundless.

I found solace in books. One of the new ones which interested me greatly was Alice Bailey's 'Reappearance of the Christ'. The notion of a Christ reborn and rediscoverable was a new one to me and it struck some deep, inner chord of awareness — I thus read the book very carefully. Mrs. C. and my mother had taken to visiting me weekly for the purposes of my further instruction, but I think they both regarded me as rather way out and off beam in my thinking, and Alice Bailey's book and my serious consideration of it, cemented this. Mrs. C. perhaps gave me up in despair at this juncture for her visits ceased abruptly, and Mother was more than usually frosty.

Another of the new books was Ramacharaka's 'Gnani Yoga'... I cannot remember its contents now, save that they included ideas on creation, dissolution, and the formless aspect of God. These sections made a peculiar impact on my mind, and I lay sleepless for a long time the night I first read it, trying to assimilate the vastness of the concepts presented. They gave me an odd sensation, and mentally I recoiled in fear.

Suddenly, I was deluged with blankness — nothing was there but vast, empty space. I was a little speck caught up in nothingness... A ghastly abyss opened before me, and I was alone, utterly alone... outside the universe, outside time, outside myself. It was unbelievably terrifying, and undeniably real. Breathlessly, I struggled back to everyday things — the safe, steady tick of the clock, the warmth of the bed, the firm solidity of Patrick's back. I do not know how long the experience lasted, perhaps only a moment of time, but it seemed an eternity, and the stark horror of it lingered into the next few days.

A third book, even more important to me in an indirect sense, was Maurice Nicholl's 'The New Man', found in the city library. This led me to 'The Mark' and 'Living Time' by the same author, and from these I learned of the work of Gurdjieff and Ouspensky. The same library yielded 'In Search of the Miraculous' and 'The Fourth Way', both by Ouspensky, which struck new roots deep into my questing mind. I saw suddenly that the entire process of evolution was geared to the increase of consciousness, and all else was incidental. This marked a definite stage in my mental apprenticeship, and my ability to comprehend increased with rapidity after this.

The cheque for Victoria Road duly arrived, but Patrick made no mention of the promised fifty pounds. I waited hopefully a day or two, thinking it had slipped his mind, and then I became anxious and asked for it. He said, very reasonably, that he could not afford to give it to me with all his current commitments. I accepted this, and replied that I didn't mind not having fifty, but could I please have twenty-five? The answer was no. Unhappily I had unwisely anticipated in advance already, and bought skirt materials for myself and Teresa and other things too, placing them on Patrick's business account at a local store. I now had to reveal this. Worse still was a guilty secret I dared not mention at all.

Some months back, before the episode of the £25, I had borrowed £10 from my mother for household expenditure which she had been in no hurry to have returned; but I had told her of the promised fifty, intending to repay it now from this. I felt very badly over this money, not having mentioned it to Patrick as I feared his reaction. My difficulties were due to a slow accummulation of deficit at the rate of a few shillings each week, the housekeeping money not stretching adequately for all it had been required to do.

I now told Mother what had happened. She said, very firmly, that it did not matter about repaying the money, but it was my duty before God to have no secret from my husband, and I must tell him of what I had done. Not being at all sure that this was good advice, I nevertheless took my courage in hand and informed Patrick of my debt. His rage was titanic and petrifying. I had "shamed him" before his in-laws. I had "gone behind his back" to deceive him. I had "betrayed" him utterly. All my frightened explanations were useless. He did not hear them, nor did he wish to.

Straight to the bank he went in a black fury, and threw down £25 on his return, commanding I repay my mother at once — and then for three days he would not speak to me at all, maintaining a stony silence on which my emotions broke again and again, so overwhelmed was I with my disgrace.

Gradually he thawed, perhaps remembering how hard I had worked, or perhaps for other reasons, for after this things were suddenly normal. At my request he put up the trellis I bought to screen the worst of the dereliction, and lay the turf I had ordered, and dug up the beaten earth of the rear garden for me to plant out — well, half of it anyway; the rest was left as a wilderness playground for the children — and thankfully once more we were friends.

The garden became my joy. The soil was rich and black and must once have been well-used, for my plants grew prolifically in the summer sunshine and I would inspect their colourful glory several times each day and even talk to them — much to my overlord's amusement. But it was infinitely better than his anger.

In July I had a rapturous experience. One night I became conscious in sleep of that which motivated me... without substance or form I hastened to meet my Beloved; without eyes to see I saw from every angle — without limbs to feel I knew vibrant warmth from light more radiant than the sun... My soul poured out in exaltation my love for Him — but alas, I awoke without memory of finding Him at last...

August brought yet another vivid dream. A nun stood before me, looking intently into my face. We were in the centre of Arbury Estate, outside the new school, and I knew she was going to give some lectures which I was to attend. Several times she spoke to me, but my thoughts were distracted from her words by my children, with whom I seemed greatly preoccupied. At length, being reassured of their safety, I turned to listen. The nun looked me full in the eyes and said firmly and clearly — "You are coming to a time of panic." My voice faltered as I replied, "Is it my panic, or the world's?" More gently came her answer, "It is yours; this is the path you had to come by. When you need help, and need help you will, call on me — I am here always. My name is Sister

Shepherd." I awoke with her voice in my ears, her calm, beautiful eyes still imaged in my memory. I felt uneasy, but gradually this subsided and I dismissed it from my mind.

In August too, came a valued experience that affected me deeply. On the twenty-second I was present at the birth of a baby girl, the child of a young woman with whom I had become acquainted. It happened apparently by chance, for I called not knowing the child was already on its way, and as there was no-one else to help at the time, the midwife asked for my assistance. The subsequent hours produced in me a strange sense of awe and a profound awareness of the mystery of human existence. I felt the whole episode held a symbolic parallel in my own life, a synchronicity that just then I could not quite place.

It was now September, and 31 was almost ready for occupation. Ironically it was still unsold, as was the Swavesey bungalow. So Patrick placed for sale our house in Histon Road, which found an immediate purchaser, and meant we must go back again to Richmond Road. In one sense I did not mind this — though I could raise no enthusiasm for the house at all; for Patrick had provisionally agreed to buy a building plot on Arbury Estate. It was in part of the new development adjacent to Roseford Road, and I was already hopefully drafting plans.

At last something constructive appeared in sight — a home in a place where I actually wanted to *be*, and a more stable material situation that would release us from the wheel of continual moves. I was now thirty years old, and my inner life (unknown to me then) was about to accelerate, paving the way for the onset of three years of intensive preparation — which would bring me into readiness for a major predestined event.

But first came '31'. A time of applied, interior impetus. A time to grow.

PART 2

FRAMEWORK FOR TUITION

You have to realise
that it is his guidance
that keeps you on the path,
and not your own strength.

Hakim Sanai, 'The Walled Garden of Truth'
translated by David Pendlebury,
Octagon Press Ltd. 1974 p. 14.

Hard the Way is,
Rough and stony,
See, I weep each time I fall —
I am feeble, lacking courage,
Fain would I not
Go at all.

The first thing to happen, before we had even unpacked, was a bursting light-bulb which mercifully shattered just as the children left the room. It set the tone of the next six months, and the strange and occult events which encompassed me.

The house was rather dark in aspect at the rear, its garden forlornly narrow and of course, completely derelict; but the new decorations were particularly pretty (I had helped with these too!) and partially made up for other frustrations, such as the loss of my flourishing plants. Teresa changed schools and settled, though less happily, in one nearer, but it worried me daily to see David disappear into the autumn mists to cross the busy roads to St. Luke's.

I was aware now of a change in my inner polarity — a deepening and widening of consciousness, and an upsurge of struggling aspiration that did not affect in the least my everyday contacts with others, but which nevertheless drew me increasingly into a solitary place within myself. Something in me seemed to quicken at this time, the restless 'seeking' grew stronger and more intense — I wanted knowledge, yes, and understanding — but more than anything I yearned for guidance and contact with the source of all my promptings. I cried out desperately in my heart again and again to be shown the way. The choked and overgrown fount of my girlhood's poesy burst forth suddenly anew, and I strove inadequately to express in words the light that at times beat upon me, and the utter desolation and despair experienced when it was withdrawn.

I dreamed one night very vividly of Patrick and myself crossing a wide tract of burning wasteland. He trundled a huge truck laden with old coffins behind him, and I walked beside him wearing a white dress and urging him on through the stark scenery and over scorching earth. My aim was to reach a cabin on the edge of the wasteland, and at length we arrived there, utterly exhausted. Two Angelic Beings stood at a turnstile and led Patrick through to the sunlit country beyond. I knew then that my responsibility for his wellbeing had ended, and other things awaited me, and woke feeling perplexed by the strange vividity of impressions and their total incomprehensibility.

Increasingly in sleep I knew that I glimpsed certain things destined to occur in my life — but the way my brain translated them rendered these perceptions little short of impossible. They simply *could not* happen. There was no conceivable situation in which they could manifest, and I clamped down on such impressions, not knowing how to store them without detriment to my mundane life, which remained as restricted as before.

Certain dream insights registered themselves as formulations or even allegories, and appeared intelligent attempts to structure some means of explanation. One such was of a massive bagatelle board with small groups of colourless, inactive figures spaced all over it. Patrick and I were the projected 'balls', which hurtled propulsively but methodically about the board when released, and were thus precipitated into the groups sequentially one by one, each impact animating its particular group into colour and action — as if the tableau represented an event that at once sprang into existence. Therefore these events or situations were already contained embryonically in Time, though latent and inoperative — requiring only contact or proximity for activation. We both entered the same 'stills', but our experiences were completely different, likewise our reactions.

And there lay our only freewill — in our reactions; and even these were governed by what we inherently *were* — what we had made of ourselves already in some absolutely specific past by former reactions and responses.

I could not know then that many of the perceptions I registered were factual. It would not have been possible for me to believe this, for I was bound in a cocoon of limitation — made small and weak and helpless, and the unwinding of this in the form of curtailed opportunity, setbacks, frustrations and hurts, taught me slowly and surely to harness my energies interiorly, and build a ladder to span the void between this imperfect reflection, life, and its perceived Supernal Reality.

I intend to record factually the salient points that came next, without attempting to interpret them — at least in the main — for I did not then understand myself what was happening, though I made many surmisals, some of which were correct as far as they went. I had to wait until 1977 for the key to these intervening years of experience, and I learned then the 'reason why' for everything that had puzzled me before.

Having ordered several books, I dreamt before they arrived that I was holding one in my hand. The cover showed no title but depicted a starry sky and a planet. I knew it held something I needed.

The books were delivered by post the following morning, and one, 'The Dark Star' by Lord Dowding, oddly enough was jacketed with the picture of my dream. With considerable expectation I read it almost immediately... and felt very disappointed. It was a spiritualist book, good of its kind, but merely confirming what I knew already, or had read elsewhere and still was not sure about. But it did contain three addresses, and I wrote to each one requesting the literature of the organisation referred to, namely The Theosophical Society, The White Eagle Lodge, and The Arcane School, none of which had been encountered formerly.

I soon learned that the Theosophical Society had been founded by Madame Blavatsky, whose major work 'The Secret Doctrine' I quickly realised was the source book for all the smaller works on similar lines already chanced upon. The White Eagle Lodge was a soundly based Centre whose founder, Grace Cooke, was a medium of the highest integrity; and The Arcane School I discovered to my surprise had been the life-effort of Alice Bailey, Madame Blavatsky's pupil, whose book had so greatly interested me. This latter was the key I sought, or so I believed.

With a newly cashed long-term insurance policy, I sent for books from all three organisations, and at the same time commenced the lengthy and detailed application necessary for a would-be student of the Arcane School. For the past year I had studied intensively every spare minute — though this largely confined itself to an hour or so every evening while the children slept and Patrick was out; but each stream of thought encountered had one vital factor in common; they all taught the relationship of pupil and teaching Master, and I became increasingly conscious of all this implied.

My mother reacted violently to my newest studies. She tolerated most of the 'lesser lights' — indeed, suffered them on her own bookshelves, but H.P.B. and Alice Bailey she could not endure. As we now lived again in the same road we usually saw each other every day, and her increasing hostility placed an even greater strain on our relationship.

I cared deeply for my mother, respected her judgement and her generally excellent mediumship — but her range of experiences and mine were totally different. What I saw as light, she saw as darkness; and though I appreciated her 'light' for its intrinsic value, it did not satisfy me. Nor did my acceptance of its validity interfere in any way with my own concepts — both were parts of a whole. But I was alone in my viewpoint; my mother's experiences were acceptable to known sources, that is, spiritualist ones, and mine apparently were not. It was considered by these authorities that I had not yet made the grade.

During this period I dreamed very consciously and frequently, and the dreams were strangely potent. In one I stood in a forest by a peat-bog, wearing the coat and hood I had worn at school as a senior pupil. I observed a replica of myself, in the same uniform, sinking gently down into the mire. Without concern I said quietly, "Kate is in the peat-bog," as if this was by intent.*

In another, I was in a small cottage, apparently my own, which was spotlessly clean and completely bare. I knew it had been 'swept and garnished'. Outside the back door was a large communal compound of beaten earth, and in the centre stood a small, blackened tree-stump. I walked over to inspect it, and as I looked, a thornbush started to grow from its root, and rapidly increased in size, moving swiftly towards me. I turned and ran back to my house, straight through the back door — but before I could close it the thornbush pushed inside — I made for the front door and ran down the road, but the bush grew right through my house and followed me. Suddenly I knew it was useless to run as I could not escape — it was required of me to accept this. So I stood still, and the bush stopped growing, and a small pig ran out from its depth and headed towards me. I let it come, and at this point I awoke.

*My only knowledge of peatbogs was that the mummified remains of early man had been found in them.

In yet a third dream I was in Russia, at the midway part of the last century. There was an epidemic of scarlet fever, and I was a nurse and therefore expected to give assistance. A young woman was brought to me, flushed crimson and burningly hot, and I felt a sudden fear of catching her fever and ran out into the open countryside. Many people were also fleeing the city, hoping to escape contagion. I thought — "flight is useless, these people are carrying the contagion with them," and I turned round and went back. I now stood in a large hall with many peasants, all frightened of the raging pestilence. I knew they had no hope but myself, and if I would not look after them, things would go badly when the fever struck. I suddenly found courage, and held out my hand, saying "I am a nurse. I heal..." and my hand glowed luminously blue. I then saw a future projection of this nurse in a long, rather primitive ward, moving from bed to bed and placing her hand on each occupant. A small brown-skinned man, like Mahatma Ghandhi, appeared from behind a screen; he smiled at me as if pleased, and read from the book he was holding — "And when she healed, she knew such exaltation..." and I awoke.

Fourthly, I was with my white-robed Guardian, who led me through the sky on winged feet, over a section of beautiful and dearly familiar country. I longed, longed, longed to go down to visit it again and find once more the loved people and places I had once known. My Companion said quietly, "Don't go down, it is not as you remember it —" but the longing drew me, and I found myself running, running through green fields towards I knew not what, with such joy and gladness. Then I stopped, bewildered and afraid. Soldiers were everywhere — an army of occupation had established itself, and my familiar haunts and loves were no more. Griefstricken, I returned.

One morning in December as we sat talking, someone suddenly looked at me through my mother's eyes. It was as though another entity had temporarily entered her body and sat regarding me with undisguised hatred and contempt. I was dreadfully shocked; the entity was strangely familiar — some part of me knew who (or what) it was, and why it had come. I felt a sharp tensing in my stomach region, and then it seemed a cord, or something similar, was severed between my mother and myself. In a few seconds it was over, and we were normal again. Mother knew someone had overshadowed her, but she said it was a benign spirit who wished to protect her from the influences I insisted on contacting, so the link between us had been psychically broken.

Perhaps I should mention that my mother had previously, on one occasion in the past year, been troubled by an unnerving visitation that sought to influence her and invade her will (not when with me), and I had several times since been aware of some remnant from this around her. She did not appear to connect the two incidents, probably because Mrs. E., on consultation, had assured her authoritatively that the episode was an initiatory 'trial' — also perhaps because I did not describe what I experienced, not wishing to upset her.

A few days after this I developed influenza, and whilst recovering, sat up in bed during the evening and tried to read. There was a curious tension in the room which affected me increasingly, and soon my inner vision produced alarming glimpses of a most repulsive entity. My energy drained from me as if the valve of a tap had been opened, and my mind became progressively numb. In sudden terror I grasped that my lifeforce was being sapped by the entity, who sought to use it, and also to enter my mindfield for some purpose of its own. For a few moments I fought it strenuously, and the battle of wills was horribly real. At the moment of greatest peril, the balance was tipped, and my own will reasserted; but through this distressing, indeed paralysing experience, I learned that only in the direst extremity are we able to put forth *any* effort of will *at all* — it requires *immense* concentration and a totally one-pointed impetus; also our *sole safeguard* in all such situations, and at all times, is to call upon the Master without cease.

What troubled me most about this was *why* it had been allowed to happen — *why* I had seemingly undergone it alone. I already knew that my path followed a predestined pattern, doubtless with minor possibilities of change, but it was frightening to think that it could be upheaved or interfered with by an alien agency. It was many years before I saw that this, and the later recorded episode, were deliberately introduced into my life; for apart from the purposes served, they helped to establish certain awarenesses, recognitions, and strengths which were essential for the future.

Even my small daughter had an unpleasant experience, either this night or the one following, as she told me in due course — insisting a "witch's hand" had clutched at her bedroom curtains when she abruptly awoke in the night, and frightened her dreadfully. She naturally knew nothing of my own experience.

My Arcane School application was accepted late in December. I had written twenty-seven close-lined pages, pouring out my limited knowledge and fumbling efforts and aspiration — and the door was opened. I thought I had come at last to the place of teaching so often glimpsed in my dreams, and studied Alice Bailey's books with diligence.

Throughout November and December, my psychic awareness became very pronounced. Every night I would waken to see symbols hanging in the air before me, large and solid and beautifully coloured. They would remain there for some moments, then gradually fade, and there was absolutely no possibility of mistaking them nor of dismissing them as imagination. The symbols themselves held meaning and related to my inner development. One, for instance, was of a young unbroken colt bucking wildly with an Indian on its back (the North American type); but the reins were firmly held, and there was no doubt who would gain control. Another was of an express train accelerating at high speed — this also emitted such a loud, dynamic sound, it was incredible to me that the whole house did not hear it.

On a third occasion I was conscious that I could see from every angle, as if I had hundreds of eyes all over my head, including the part that lay on the pillow — and *all* the eyes could see the solitary, luminous object which hung high in the room near the ceiling. It seemed a new faculty developed within me. I felt I was growing a powerful central organ of vision.

Sometimes a faintly luminous figure stood by my bed, and once I wakened in the winter dark to find the blue-robed nun I had seen long ago, so close I could see the folds of her gown, and apparently as real and solid as myself. She emanated love and serenity, and I registered telepathically that her name was Teresa.

Another time I woke to find a parcel there — large, sturdy, and wrapped in very unmetaphysical brown paper. For a moment I was so sure it was 'real' that I reached out my hand to touch it, but even as I moved it faded away. This phenomenon was unlike former symbols in that it was static, whereas the hanging objects had glided slightly. Somewhat irrationally I felt again the now familiar pang of apprehension.

In general these insights and perceptions were of a positive nature, and I knew that they were there simply as signals — the side-effects of an interior working that was much more important than the experiences themselves. They undoubtedly caused a certain amount of strain, for in the midst of a normal, routine life it is disconcerting to 'see things' repeatedly, and sometimes it was all too much for me. Night after night I *saw* and experienced, and my head felt overstimulated with the frequency of registration. I turned to Patrick for comfort and the balance of his everyday normality, but soon realised the impossibility of communication, particularly with someone who most assuredly did not wish to know.

We had passed through a bleak period just before Christmas. Patrick was never at his best on such festive occasions and he also resented the extra expenditure Christmas involved. This had caused me much heartache in the past as my family have always celebrated Christmas in the traditional manner, and the children naturally loved the gifts and the atmosphere and so did I. His irritation and depression were accentuated by the fact that the Swavesey bungalow was still unsold, and most of his capital and a bank loan were tied up in it, though he remained convinced that it would sell as soon as spring arrived. In addition to this the plans submitted for the new house had been queried, and were now held up by planning authorities who took long vacations between sessions at this time of the year, and Patrick had no work at all unless he dared proceed without consent. There was in this case little likelihood of trouble; the house was similar to others on the estate, and the query had concerned the height of roof elevations, not the actual structure; but he was thoroughly gloomy and out of temper.

I felt particularly despairing through matters already referred to, and wondered now if I could really continue much longer to shore up our marriage, which gave so little for the work put into it and was so frequently unrewarding. At the peak of a miserable episode, when I felt the end had been reached, and my endurance exhausted — a spirit, like an Angel, wrapped me round in an essence of love one tear-filled night, and passed it through me to Patrick who lay asleep by my side... and I perceived with wonder that the hard shell he had built around him silently shattered, dissolved, and melted away.

I am not sure if he had any awareness of change. He may have done, and suppressed it as he did with other awarenesses later; but he was better for some while after this, and went back to work cheerfully and without qualm — an action that proved justified.

The meditation exercises outlined by the Arcane School were religiously embarked upon at the beginning of January. Never having meditated before, I found it surprisingly difficult to still my nervous system, pounding heart, and wayward mind. There seemed to be a blockage somewhere — my normally excellent ability to visualise deserted me, and I had a hard struggle to concentrate. Unaccountably I felt depressed, and the books I read did not help this. The 'Secret Doctrine' was ponderous and wordy and its study was not made easier by my mother's repeated assertions that it was 'black' — meaning it had undesirable emanations. This was dutifully confirmed by Mrs. C., but knowing their biases I read on stubbornly, forcing out of my consciousness the dark fear that had begun to hover on the edge of my perception.

I tried other books by recommended authors (all Theosophical) though without alleviation of whatever ailed me. Concurrent with these I continued my efforts to comprehend the work of Alice Bailey, to whose teaching I was strongly drawn. The books held truth, of this I was certain, yet here and there, in some of the later works especially, were comments I found difficult to assimilate, and I was sorely puzzled.

In the midst of my probing, a vivid dream affected me with its dual sense of consolation and awareness of trial. I was in a Church which was almost empty as the service had not yet begun, and I felt desperately lonely and unhappy. An old man with youthful agility walked up the aisle and sat immediately behind me, in some way looking full into my face despite the logical impossibility of this. His own smooth features were either Chinese or Tibetan, and I had the distinct impression that I knew him, and he was, or had been, my Teacher. Suddenly I felt his hand on my right shoulder — it was strong and workworn, and channelled into me a stream of clear blue restorative power. Without sound his enigmatic words were transmitted into my mind: "Even when all seems lost... *God is still at the helm.*"

I saw then an arab tent of jet black sailcloth, erected on the edge of a rocky peninsula with the sea below. The tent seemed connected with myself, and as I looked at it, a rent appeared from top to bottom, and whatever was inside was disclosed to my view. But I could not remember what I saw — save that there was light... and I immediately awoke.

Everything in my life was going wrong but not in the usual way. I was accustomed to difficulties and setbacks, and although they were irksome there was a 'rightness' about them that inwardly made them acceptable, but a different feeling altogether surrounded the trend of present events. Foolishly, I caught my finger on a rusty nail at the back of the bookshelf, and was given an anti-tetanus injection to which I was unfortunately allergic, with much subsequent distress and discomfort before this was discovered. I dreamt I had unwittingly imbibed poison and had to have an antidote, and suspected that the physical incident, and the dream event, were both reflections of a deeper reality.

There was a further complication in that a peculiar, high-pitched note began sounding in my head at odd times and nearly drove me crazy. I linked this, unreasonably, with the potent current that appeared to stem from the School. Yet it was ridiculous to think this way — there was so much truth here, how could it be other than beneficial?

One morning after days of fruitless meditative effort I at last felt calm and at peace, and was conscious of light and a real reaching into myself. During a moment when my entire concentration was focussed to a point, I became aware that someone was gazing into my head from above. His face was reflected, as if in a mirror, *inside* the cranial region, and I perceived it from the point of focussed attention poised a little higher in location — yet he was peering *into my eyes*, though I knew he looked down from the back of my head.

I saw his features with crystal clarity. He was a young Indian (from the continent of India) with a light skin, brown eyes, and a broad strip of white material bound about his forehead. I knew, in the breathless stillness of his visitation, that he observed and noted everything in my condition in less than an instant, and I emerged, astonished, but strangely happy. This was the sole constructive happening since my linkage with the School, and I felt it concerned only myself and not the organisation.

My mother's hostility continued to grow, though without any foundation externally as I did not speak to her of my doubts, being reluctant to acknowledge them even to myself. She was grimly opposed to Alice Bailey, and harshly condemnatory of her School. I tried to ignore her comments, convinced her assessments were unobjective — yet her words held a warning ring of truth that created an inner conflict. It was like walking through a dark maze. I knew I had found a facet of the truth, however unacceptable to my mother, and I was loathe to let it go.

Now came a frighteningly lucid dream in which I was acutely aware of instruction. No attempt was made at formulation — I simply observed. I saw a large Queen Bee buzzing loudly in an office. She suddenly crashed headlong into a wall and fell to the floor, a swarm of wasps immediately superceding her. I then stood in a museum which opened onto a street, its ceiling hung with all manner of disused farming implements. Someone obliged me to look carefully up at them, and I noted that all were worn-out and outmoded.

Along each wall was ranged an assortment of sinks and wash-basins, all of which were stained in varying degrees particularly around the waste outlets. These, too, were old and disused, with the silent aura of abandonment. Next door was an old-fashioned shop — an outdated perambulator standing by the window. I glanced at the baby it held and was shocked, for its face was aged and oriental, and markedly distorted. Further along the street a terrible accident had occurred; a haywaggon had overturned and people were crushed beneath it... I awoke feeling sick and alarmed.

Twenty-eight days from the commencement of the meditation work, a final shock was administered. During a meditation I saw clairvoyantly the symbol of an ass wearing a red hat (mockery), followed by the most hideous distortion of the figure of Christ. I stopped at once. The dark shadow had now fully entered my horizon. Broken and grieved, I could no longer ignore the signs thrust upon me, knowing beyond doubt an adverse element was present that ought not to be there.

That night the situation climaxed. I lay in a semi-conscious, almost anaesthetised state, but not really asleep, and watched a powerful, mis-shapen oriental form driven out from my aura by One unseen. It seemed to take a long time, and twice was ejected only to return, but the third time was cleared completely, and I was conscious of a deep relief and inner comfort. Months afterwards it occurred to me, rightly or wrongly, that I was used as a kind of magnet to draw this entity for its subsequent release and benefit. It was a comforting thought.

After this sobering experience I packed all my newest, most cherished books and sent them to a London bookshop for sale secondhand, feeling I must cease this line of study for the time being. They had cost me twenty pounds and I received six in exchange. A bitter pill, its implications of error rubbed in from the financial angle by Patrick, and the spiritual by Mother, who was condescendingly kind in her triumphant 'rightness'.

I remembered the parcel seen by my bed — identical in size and appearance with the one so recently despatched, and dimly grasped that the whole episode had been placed before me for some purpose as yet uncomprehended. I noticed too, with chagrin, that many of the returned titles my mother had so strenuously deemed 'black' still rested on her bookshelves — apparently uncontaminated as were mine. Both recollection and observation caused deep emotional turmoil, and I questioned constantly what I had done to bring upon myself such an appalling experience.

Was there indeed an 'army of occupation'? Was the pearl no longer in the setting I had found it in before? Thinly veiled memories from the long distant past coalesced in my mind with the present and I was uncertain and confused. I dreamt I stood in the street at night, by a dhuni fire, watching several persons who sat cross-legged around its dying embers. The remains of the thorn-pig lay in the centre, blackened and almost gone. Something had been burned out — but whether from my own past karma or some other source, I did not then know.

The wound went deep and humiliation brought me low. I saw starkly my own emptiness — my lack of knowledge and understanding, concluding wearily that all my efforts had been in vain. But from beneath it all... came peace. In the innermost depths a sweet and gentle essence bathed my soul, and crept upon me almost unawares. There was no reproach... no admonition. For three days I was held in the stillness and love of another's Presence, and knew the Reality of His existence more surely than ever before.

For three nights also a strange phenomenon repeated just as I reached the point of sleep... twice I scarcely grasped this sufficiently in my brain to remember, but on the third night its registration was consciously clear. I stood in a minute square in the apex of my head — less than a pinpoint in size, yet seemingly of normal height. On a raised dais before me sat a small man, crosslegged, in Persian robes of the softest and most delicate hues. Gently He smiled upon me, remaining perfectly still and without speaking, his face calmly compassionate and expressing an indescribable sweetness and humility.

I knew I had been allowed to enter His presence for some purpose, and that He was *permitting* me to see Him and to retain the memory. I knew too, beyond any possibility of query, that He was my Teacher, and I had 'found' Him at last.

I realise now in retrospect that the dream of the Queen Bee with all its related data, clearly conveyed information about Madame Blavatsky's work and its issue, the Theosophical Society. It also referred to Alice Bailey's.

There are old thought-forms connected with the meditation work of occult schools that are still impregnated with the mental substance of those that created them, and to which have been added the projections of newer, perhaps less carefully selected pupils. Such formations, if inherently contaminated by imprints karmicly associated with magical ritual, egotistical desires, sensuality, or the evocation of power, would draw to them elementals and discarnate entities with similar impressions. These can activate the thoughtforms with unpleasant results, and constitute a very real danger to the trusting and ignorant would-be student.

It must also be borne in mind that the methods and teaching materials of all such schools are always discarded after a time (assuming they were authentic in the first place) and for this reason, and a fresh outpouring of tuition instigated elsewhere. Though much information can be gleaned from a study of their literature — as in the case of the prolific output of Alice Bailey, any existent element of distortion, if undetected, can offset the knowledge gained; and the developmental mechanism, either written or practical, of outdated educational impulses should *without exception* be approached with very great caution. For safe and effective tuition, a living, *genuine* Teacher is essential, and this cannot be overstated.

Amongst the experiences of that fateful January was one in particular of a type unencountered before or since. It was precognitive and quite stunning in its effect, occurring early one morning when almost time to get up. I lay awake, my mind quiescent, and a box like an old-fashioned peepshow was placed over my eyes, and I was at once projected into the living scene inside.*

**NOTE.* These numerous symbolic insights and dreams have been included to enable their outworking to be traced by anyone sufficiently interested. The more significant precognitions will be seen to reflect on several levels throughout the trilogy, and not all can be found in their most purposeful mode of externalisation in Book 1 (Signals from Eternity).

This was a barren, rocky terrain on which stood a lighthouse — and I found myself in a tiny bare room at the top, in which I lived. Below I saw Patrick, collecting and carrying fuel. Backwards and forwards he went, upstairs and down, with heavy buckets of coal. Working and working, and so intent on his task he seemed unconscious I was there. And I knew, suddenly, it was through him I was in this bleak, inhospitable place.

I looked from a narrow window at the approach route; nearby loomed a large Victorian building in darkness, with shuttered windows and a tattered board faintly worded 'Dr. Mortimer's School'. It was obviously empty and non-functioning, wreathed in a heavy atmosphere of gloom. A signpost stood in the road, well-lit and starkly clear against the sky. Amazed, my eyes scanned the signs spaced out upon its length from bottom to top — which named each place of consequence in my life, including the first firm I worked for, and concluding at the top with an arm inscribed in black on ochre yellow. It read, 'Arcane School'.

Between the post and the lighthouse was a stretch of desolate, twilit, boulder-strewn sand. I turned away, appalled, and peered through the window opposite, from where the view was even worse. Twisted grey rocks lay in grotesque shapes on the moonlit shore, and in the distance heaved a black and threatening sea. Terrified, I struggled to wake, knowing the peepshow scene was a constructed illusion; and just as I emerged, I glimpsed the lighthouse again from a distance. It was old and immensely strong, vividly etched against the sombre skyline with three bricks missing from its upper parapet. I understood simultaneously that it represented myself, and the missing bricks were incidents in time.

Momentarily I also understood the imagery of the whole; that it was a glyph containing the essence of the training process before me — beset with karmic elements, not necessarily my own — that were destined to gather force and break about my head with increasing velocity — strengthening me by degrees for my preordained contact years later with the 'sea' itself.

In surfacing from the potent effect of the 'peepshow', I registered in an intuitive flash that I would have to live in Swavesey, a factor which concerned me far more than the foregoing at that time, for unbelievable though it was, it was uncomfortably relevent to my then-current life.

This particular perception soon sank peaceably into my subconscious. It did not seem feasible, and I put it from my mind.

Spring was coming, house sales would boom again, and my lovely new home in St. Alban's Road was now well under way.

A curious adjunct to this experience was a glimpse from another life — not into it, but *from* it, as if it reflected into this one — for I saw a woman and a child whom I remembered. Both wore Victorian dress, and the child, a little girl, was Henriette — a niece, I think, whom I had loved, and who died of a fever. They were peering 'down' at me from a region that linked two stratas, their dimension and this one. There was a rush of memory, vivid glimpses of Victorian England, and a confusion of impressions of India — then a wistful contralto voice singing a song of the day (or so I assume):

'Don't go away my love,
Won't you please stay, my love,
Please come back
Oh, please come back
To me...'

As the last notes died away the impressions abruptly faded and could not be recalled. Only the song with its plaintive intonations remained in my memory, and has lingered there ever since.

On February 17th, I again dreamed with unprecedented clarity, and this brought with it a feeling of joy. I was in a vast schoolroom which appeared to contain the whole world, and sat in a certain place near the aisle — my own place, which was never changed. A Teacher sat on a raised wooden ledge high above the classroom — and told us there was a race to be run, a goal to achieve, and a prize to be gained. There were only two rules to abide by — we must sing, and run, all the way. With the rest of the class I entered the aisle, and strove to move along the prescribed route — but it was so heavily crammed with people that movement was maddeningly difficult and slow. No-one was singing and very few made any attempt to run. I could not understand this, and tried my hardest to run despite the crush.

As we rounded a corner, the crowd suddenly thinned and at last I could move. All at once the way cleared, and I found myself right out in front of the rest, facing a long, clear stretch that led 'home'. At its commencement, two persons in authority were stationed — and none passed this point save at their behest. Myself and six or seven others met at the touchline, still marking time with our feet; then we began to run in earnest; I waited for someone to sing, but nobody did, and finding myself at the front, quaveringly my voice rose on its own... the others then joined me, but my voice was not strong or very sure, and they all sang at different pitches and varying speeds.

When the song was ended we ran a short way in silence, then I called out, "Who will sing this time?". There was no answer, and twice again I repeated the words with the same result. So I sang once more on my own, less nervously now... and they all drew close to my heels and began to sing in unison...

Many onlookers lined the aisle — some booed and jeered us, some applauded. Some stood with heads averted, silent, but with listening ears, and I knew it was for these latter that we sang. Again the song came to an end, and this time everyone stopped, for here the clear road ended and only a narrow lane led onwards.

I noticed that many small gifts were held by those that ran with me, and when I urged them on, they said they had received the promised rewards, and the race was finished; but I felt it had not, and continued alone along the narrow pathway. On one side was the wooden ledge the Teacher had been raised on, high and forbidding above my head, and on the other lay a deep black abyss against a blank, white screen.

Waveringly I commenced a new song — one that I cannot now remember; my voice was feeble and I was afraid, and very conscious of my loneliness. Gradually it gathered strength, and as I ran, I became aware that I was growing, and my limbs were firm and strong, and my voice clear and resonant and ringing. I heard voices calling me, encouraging me through the darkening gloom to a light which lay ahead. Suddenly I rounded a bend and found myself in the familiar classroom — but now a welcoming group awaited me with singing and banners and much jubilation. And there, in the centre of the throng, sat my Master, His arms held wide. Someone dearly loved rose to greet me, and handed me the promised prize — it was a silver lighthouse with a circular disc inside it, like a lens. I knew that if I peered within I should see 'Time' — past, present and future, not in a clairvoyant sense, but from the unlimited state beyond illusion.

Since December Teresa had suffered various childhood ailments, and in March, alarmed me by producing a very high fever which would not subside. There was Scarletina at school, and our doctor thought she may have picked up the germ which had not externalised properly in a rash. For four days she lay between life and death, and during this dreadful period I dreamt she fell down on the new Estate, and I lifted her crying, "My baby, my baby," to see her eyes close…

In fear I woke immediately, and rushed to the bathroom and retched. I knew beyond doubt that many of my dreams were precognitive and my fears can be imagined. Yet it was not so. The fever passed, leaving her thoroughly depleted for almost two months — in which time her temperament adjusted itself from the passive, gentle baby she had been, to an imperious little girl. Of her own accord she changed the spelling of her name, and significantly kept it this way for several years.

I knew of the transition to ego-consciousness which always occurs around this time, though usually less obviously, and comforted myself that this was what I had seen symbolically. But three years later the dream manifested, not in death most mercifully, but slight concussion from a fall at school, through which she spent five days in hospital.

Prior to this episode I had always feared losing a child, and believed the fear belonged to a former life when this had happened; but after facing it again in my dream, the fear dispersed, and I was freed from it in its strongest form.

With the six pounds from the sale of my books, I decided to invest in further study. There was a brief reference in one of the White Eagle Lodge books (which were still retained) to a course in Astrology, and I sent for it, to Patrick's vexation, as he felt I had no regard for the value of money. The course was a clear and excellent series of articles on chart erection and delineation, the second practice chart being one's own natus. My own birthchart gave me a faint sense of shock, I did not know why; it was as if some part of me understood it and attempted to register it on my brain, and I felt a fleeting joyous anticipation — but when the time came to interpret it my reassurance dissolved.

There were potentialities, yes, but powerful conflicts, discords and difficulties to harmonise and control. Struggle and heartbreak, loneliness and scandal were written there — and potent illumination of such strength that it created problems. I decided to complete the course before probing further, hoping my judgements would prove too hasty.

In April, '31' was put for sale pending the hoped-for move, and a first-day viewer bought it gleefully. I could hardly wait for the change in circumstance, and selected colour schemes and arranged our furnishings in my mind to speed the great day. But Patrick was worried, for the bungalow at Swavesey remained unsold and most of his capital was still locked up in it. He had dropped the price, already low, and it was an absolute bargain; but people rarely looked over it — it was too rurally situated for most tastes — a fact I could well appreciate. Our current house-sale would only partially solve the dilemma — it was well-mortgaged for a start, and Patrick could buy no further land and would soon be workless unless a purchaser could speedily be found.

One morning as I walked from the local shops towards home, he drew up beside me in the van in a state of suppressed excitement. A young Bank Manager had approached him on site, and made him an excellent offer for the new house, too good really to turn down — but he *had* turned it down, of course, because it was *my* house...

I looked at him, my heart sinking. There was a question in his eyes behind the anxiety and acquiescence. His finances were desperately strained, and he knew I was always concerned for him. Everything in me rose and protested. Of course it was *my* house — mine! Mine! Worked for, hoped for, promised... It was in the right place — I *knew* it was. The place that was part of my destiny...

It was no use. I could not do it to him. He hadn't my resilience, nor faith, and the strain of over-long worry was wearing him down. I knew my alternative was the bungalow itself — there was no time left for anything else. I remembered my dream of Victoria Road, and the by-lane with the rural scenery — "This is the route you must take..." Patrick still stood there, eager, unpushing, waiting my response. He was again the young, enthusiastic man I had married. "Take me to Swavesey," I said at length, "and let me see the bungalow again."

We went that afternoon. It had been raining, and a soft mist rose from the earth as the sun came out. The bungalow stood in a narrow lane outside the village, the last in the row. Beyond it, and around, stretched fields and hedges, ditches — and cows. It was very rural indeed. I didn't feel very well — my recurrent cystitis afflicted me, and I looked at the views feeling anything but joyful. The air shimmered damply above the turned earth where the drains were newly laid, and as I watched uncertainly, the earth seemed to stir and quiver with life, and I felt a sudden urge to plant it and press in new shoots to the thick clay-like soil. I knew then I must come here; that already I was committed, as impressions sought release to create a garden — in this place I had tried all along to avoid.

Patrick was overwhelmed by my decision, and sold 'my' house without delay, making arrangements at the same time to buy another plot — this time on Roseford Road itself. "You shall have this instead," he said. Yes, I thought gloomily, but it won't be ready this year.

I packed to move in a kind of daze, wondering what on earth had got into me, for I certainly did not want to go. My mother, whose life at that time was full and active, said comfortingly, "One day you'll look back on this and think it a blessing." One day maybe — but only when it was over.

The isolation was greater than before, at Histon. Here, the handful of wives in the lane all worked in the city (there were no children), and left with their husbands well before eight, as did Patrick, and no-one returned till evening. Patrick worked all hours with the light summer evenings, and then went to his pub, having taken packed meals for the day, so I only saw him late at night. Both children were at school, and I was village-bound by the appalling bus service that only ran twice a week, and if I had used it, I couldn't get back in time to collect Teresa from school, some distance away. So I lived in splendid isolation save on Tuesday mornings, when Father brought Mother by car out to visit.

Now was the time of my mother's flowering; she started a group for prayer and meditation in July and did much good work with various people. Her mediumship was sound — she sensed the dead and passed on their messages; sometimes she glimpsed the future; she could locate what was lost, give good counsel, lay-on hands for healing (most effectively), and console the bereaved. Only myself did she deal with severely. She would not take me seriously as an aspirant. I was always "not ready", "too impatient", "too young and inexperienced". Now of course I was safely tied up in Swavesey, and she relaxed and was sternly kind — until I mentioned trying to leave, then down came the clamps again.

One Tuesday morning she brought a visitor, a young woman named Rose, four years older than myself, whom she had met on a visit to the White Eagle Lodge. Rose, too, was a professional medium, sharing Mother's points of view, and already invited to her group. We liked each other, but I was nervous of her air of knowledgeability, and of her poise — and at a loss also, over the amazing fact that with three children agewise like my own, she worked part-time and was still free in the evenings to take services and attend meetings.

My days, after domestic chores were dealt with, were spent in reading and study, or working in the large field-like garden. I oscillated between two poles; one of intense personal loneliness, the other of acutely sensitised spiritual awareness. Often as I walked the lanes, fringed knee-high with meadowsweet, I would feel myself accompanied — the sense of Presence and a sympathising love so strong, it was virtually tangible. At other times I knew despair — and the sensation of abandonment. I was out on a limb, cut-off from the bustle of life — and I could not grasp why.

Having pored over Astrological books until my brain was weary, and now armed with my newly acquired skill, I proceeded to recast my birthchart and those of my children. The results made my stomach turn over. There was something ominous in each of them I could not understand, connected in each case with the positioning of either Neptune, Uranus or Pluto. According to all the books something drastic would happen, in my own case at the age of thirty-three or thirty-four as near as I could judge — either severe illness, or death, or some dreadful catastrophe.

My intuitive feelings concerning the influence of these three planets was quite different from the delineation their aspects indicated — but the eminent astrologers whose books I studied were all unanimously in accord regarding their malefic squares. Feeling sick with fear I tore up the charts, and even the Course, and left them in the empty grate. With heavy heart I went to bed; but sleep surprisingly brought comfort. I was with my children in a large car which was being driven at tremendous speed along a highway. Pinned above the windscreen were three birthcharts, and one by one my Companion explained them to me. He was gently amused by my misunderstanding, and reassured me repeatedly, pointing out certain connecting links in each chart. I could not remember his words on waking — but found afterwards that I understood grades and levels of evolution that had not been clearly registered before.

In July I had a profound experience which was difficult to retain and sort out in my mind. In sleep I was taken to what seemed the boundaries of the Universe. All Creation lay before me, spread out like a vast series of interpenetrating rays and arcs in the most exquisite shades and colours. Every planet took the likeness of a curving ray — and the ray contained its entire cycle of evolution from beginning to end; the concrete physical speck being but its focal point of consciousness moving along the ray in Time.

I saw the earth's consciousness traversing Time, and fast approaching a chasm, or spiral turn — where it must leave one phase of evolution for another. I cried out in fear, for I knew the tumult this would create — I seemed caught up in the body of the earth and rapidly hurtling towards the chasm. As I began to shriek I was lifted away, and told that I had long since 'died' to earth, and that this upheaval was not for me but for the mass of men.

I saw then that I was part of a Whole — yet in the Whole I still had my place — there were twelve in the cluster of souls to which I belonged, and they bore me, formless, yet formed, across the singing beauty of the Universe — comforting me, bearing me up, because the veils of the earth were upon me, and I could not remember whence I came. I recall vividly even now their joyousness and delightful humour, and the sense of unity and belonging, but dimly experienced and apprehended. They held me in a giant blue ray which I thought was Jupiter, and healing balm poured through the nucleus that was my consciousness. I became absorbed into the greater life encompassing me, and knew and understood that nothing is lost by such merging of identity — I had left my small self for a greater, but it was still 'I' — individuality was retained throughout, but the bounded became the boundless.

I saw my own little point in Time, and the state to which my consciousness was travelling. I saw Everything. I knew Everything, yet still the merest veil kept me from God the Absolute. Returning to normal awareness I was thrust through level after level of decreasing states of being, until the physical was reached.

In sleep there were strong intimations that we should soon leave Swavesey, but sadly there was outwardly as yet no sign of this. I had adapted quite well to the village itself, which was a very old one. It had a sense of familiarity, and several ancient houses in particular, evoked the persistent awareness of knowing them before.

Passing one of these one morning, I recalled a recurrent dream from the early days of my marriage, of being a young woman in a

Puritan-type dress, with two small children clinging to my skirts and a baby in my arms, hiding behind the door of an upper room. My husband, fleeing from cavaliers, had struggled through the window and leapt from the porch below — thence to his horse, which I heard galloping away as he left me to my fate. At that moment, three soldiers burst into the room with drawn swords, and I always awoke.

The house that stirred this memory had a large stone porch and could so easily have been the one in my dream, even to its cobbled yard — but perhaps this was simply association. I disliked the big Church and its dank gloominess, and also the cobbled market square where I felt repeatedly a 'witch' had been burned, but whether this was really so I did not find out. Mother, too, made mention of her own associative links. We both independently registered a Tudor cottage which may once have been hers... But this is a digression.

At last a potential purchaser came to view the bungalow; he beat down the price a little bit more, and then requested a second mortgage. He was a brash, conceited man, and Patrick hated him on sight, but nevertheless he agreed to sell, and on the man's terms. The problem now was where to live. We looked at several houses in the city, but there was only one that he would consider, positioned quite close to our former home. Despite my misgivings which lacked any foundation, for it was quite a pleasant house, he put in an offer for it and awaited results.

That night I had a startling dream experience in which I was shown three oblong pools, one after the other; the first was half-full, the second three-quarters full, and the third completely full of stagnant, static water. In the dream, Patrick and myself were standing with the children at the entrance to the path that led alongside the pools, and our unseen Guide spoke sternly to me, grasping my arm in warning. I turned to Patrick and said in a clear, ringing voice, "Go back! Go back! Go back!", pointing to the direction from which we had come. I awoke with the words still on my lips, alarm in my mind.

I told Patrick of the dream, despite the fact that he usually reacted strongly against my intuitions. He said nothing, but I noticed he did not follow up his offer in the usual way, and a few days later we heard that a higher bid had gone in. He left it at that.

That same week I had another dream — in which I entered a large, solid house with exceptionally well-timbered floors and woodwork. I knew this was to be mine, and stood in the centre of a sunlit upstairs room, aware that something vitally important to me was about to begin.

There seemed little likelihood of this, however, for within days the proposed purchaser had over-reached himself with Patrick, and they fell out over some required extra that the latter would not agree, so the sale was cancelled and we were back where we started.

One morning, feeling particularly disheartened and abandoned, I went into the bedroom and began to cry inconsolably, calling out in my heart to the Master and imploring Him to hear me. I tried to express the bitter loneliness of my situation and my frequent despair. How long was I to remain here? Why was I cut off from the contacts and activity of life? Where had I failed Him? The tears welled from some deep inner fount and flowed copiously. At length, worn out with crying, I rose to set about my work. Last evening's paper had been put through the door with the morning's edition, and I opened it idly, scanning without interest the 'Houses for Sale' column which was the first thing I saw. The words 'Roseford Road' were written near the top in thick capitals, followed by details of a delightful sounding property with four bedrooms, an orchard and lawns, price £4,750. My heart leapt, though the price made it quite out of the question, but my fertile brain immediately busied itself conceiving all manner of impractical ways of obtaining it.

Patrick, naturally, would not even look at the house, but so great was my insistence he consented to take me to inspect it the following evening, when I also saw the work recently commenced on his new plot — our prospective home. The house was old-fashioned but carefully built to an architect's specification, the walls inordinately solid, and woodwork throughout in polished columbian pine. The huge garden had a side entry large enough to use as a building-plot, and I mentioned this to Patrick on my return. It made no difference. It was still far more than he would pay, however great its value.

Over the weekend a young couple viewed our bungalow and said they would buy it, confirming this immediately with the agent. They were first-time buyers, and if we wanted the sale, we must move out fast. Patrick did want the sale, and we again looked at houses, several of which I would have been grateful for, but he refused each one for some reason or another.

Reluctantly, at last he agreed to look at 47, the large house I had already visited. As he went through the door he bent his head in a certain fashion that I had long recognised in him as a sign of interest. He measured the side-plot, and to my astonishment, offered the owner £4,200, a drop of £550 — and more astonishingly, she said she would consider it.

I could hardly sleep with anticipation. If the offer was refused, we should be hard-pressed to raise more. I dreamed that I was back in the house talking to the old lady. She said she would sell to us, but I was afraid to believe it. Then I found something extraordinary happening — I separated into three selves — one, solid and physical, lay sleeping on the bed, a thin cord joining her to a second self, in which my consciousness was centred. This self was quivery, unsubstantial, and afraid. On a level above me, set in a brightly lit square, I gazed upon a third self — a replica of my human form, but with a grace, assurance and dignity that I have never possessed. This higher part of me, for such I knew it to be, looked quietly upon me, the knowledge of my future destiny firmly in her grasp. I beseeched her with my eyes — please, may I have the house? She nodded, and smiled — there was a slight pause, and then she shook her head — she seemed to indicate yes, but not for long. Then my eyes became riveted to her face — a pair of spectacles grew over her features, and I knew she meant me to understand that as yet I *could not see*, the future must remain veiled to me.

She held up a little book and indicated that she wished me to study it. It was pale blue, with 'Ancient Wisdom' written in silver lettering on the cover, and a winged caduceus on its spine complete with entwined serpents. Then I was impelled again, breathless and gasping, into my physical body.

Our offer was accepted, arrangements smoothly made, and the contract quickly signed. Two weeks later, on August 14th, we moved in. The house was very dirty but I tackled it with a joyous heart. At last I had reached the place so often indicated in my dreams, and knew with certainty something was about to begin.

We jointly decorated the big house completely, from top to bottom, and the result was splendid, though physically exhausting. Patrick was again approached by a would-be purchaser — this time for the new structure, still at foundation stage, and I told him to sell it and we would stay here. Jubilant, he made arrangements to do so, and was suddenly more cheerful than for years.

In early September I dreamt that I lay on a couch in a beautiful room banked with flowers — too weary and exhausted to appreciate where I found myself. There was a sudden commotion and two women burst in upon me. One was middle-aged, and the other young and most obviously pregnant. It was rapidly made clear to me that more than this — she was about to give birth at any moment.

I rose from the couch, my tiredness gone, and led the woman into an ante-room where her child was delivered into my arms; the older woman stood by to comfort her. No sooner was the child born, when another woman entered the room in the same condition, followed by a third, both about to give birth. I awoke wondering what it could mean.

If I am mistaken: it does not matter much to your future.
But if I am right: it is all-important to your future.
...The Caliph Ali.

Idries Shah, 'The Way of the Sufi' p. 188. Octagon Press Ltd. 1968.

The children settled swiftly in our new situation, which quickly proved beneficial to us all. They both liked the new school, made new friends, and revelled in the large garden with its spacious ornamental pool and prolific orchard. The garden was a source of wonder. To actually have a garden already laid out and in order! And such a garden! Every so often I would break off from whatever I was doing and investigate the plant population. Never had I hoped to possess so much beauty, and I loved it.

The decorating took nearly six weeks and towards the end I worked quite consciously against time. It was as if I had a deadline and must be able and ready to meet it. I felt the insistent urge to contact certain others and to ask them if they would like to form a group for mutual study, but was nervous of approaching them and kept putting it off. The powerful current in my mind was puzzling, seeming out of all proportion to what I hoped to do. I had no knowledge then of the incarnate Teacher whose eye was upon us, and who used the means now activating my brain to draw certain persons into relationship, and prepare them for his entry into their lives. Towards this end I blundered blindly forward, fearful of causing offence, and unwittingly pitting myself at the same time against the obstacles of shyness, vulnerability and uncertainty within my own temperament.

At last the house was finished. My muscles ached from exertion and cried out for rest, and I felt heartily sick of work in every form. The morning after its completion, I left the breakfast dishes in the sink and went into town to catch up on the shopping. Whilst waiting for the return bus home, I heard a shout, and a young woman with a small child hurtled across the road towards me, apparently bent on getting herself and her child run down in the heavy traffic. It was Joan E., whom I had met in the pre-natal clinic before having Teresa, and who had shared the same ward when our daughters were born. She greeted me now like a long-lost friend, though our previous acquaintance had not merited this.

Several times we had met in the intervening years, until her second child, a boy, arrived, at which point we lost contact. We exchanged news of our lives in general and I let the bus go without me. Hesitantly she began to tell me of the period of great stress she had passed through, and asked how I had overcome my own post-natal difficulties. I mentioned tentatively my philosophical and aspirational studies — expecting the usual rebuff or closing up which invariably occurred when such subjects were broached. She looked at me intently, her heart in her eyes, and I think at that moment Joan and I recognised our basic kinship.

Before saying goodbye I referred to the group I was hoping to form, and gave her my address — departing rather abruptly as the next bus had arrived. The following morning she visited me early and unexpectedly, anxious to learn more. My formulations had been hazy, but thus confronted were now obliged to give themselves shape, which they did with surprising ease. On leaving, Joan said firmly that if there was to be a group, she wished to be part of it.

In my nervousness and lack of confidence in my own ability, I had asked for a sign — and I felt that Joan provided it. I wrote to the others whom I had in mind, hardly knowing them at all, and awaited events with apprehension. One replied by return of post, another telephoned, and two called separately to see me. I outlined to them my intentions, and all expressed interest — though Rose said she was not free immediately and would join us later; but the outcome was the arrangement of the first meeting for October 23rd.

Meanwhile Joan had called again, yet despite her obvious enthusiasm and our growing friendship, there seemed a reticence about her which created a subtle barrier between us. On the morning of her third visit, close on the second, I found myself telling her quite spontaneously about my neurasthenic feelings at Histon. Suddenly she reached out her hand to touch me, and as if a trigger had been released, began to pour out her own fears and the factors that lay beneath them. It was a kind of catharsis, healing in effect, and the bond between us strengthened and deepened, lifting our relationship to another level entirely.

This gentle, inner prompting to bring out aspects of my own life has happened many times since then, not without considerable embarrassment to me, for much of the substance expressed I would have preferred to keep to myself. Yet whatever the source of this impetus it well knew what it was doing, for again and again it elicited a release, often of an emotional voltage quite out of keeping with the surface personality life. It was as though memories or impressions had been stored or locked away, and needed some specially made channel of exit from which to overflow, thus deflecting an otherwise disruptive consequence.

Our first group meeting was now imminent, and sometimes I saw the funny side of my own intensity of purpose, my absolute seriousness about it all. I had prayed earnestly and repeatedly before embarking on this, not knowing why it should be of such importance to me, or why I should feel that such a very small venture had a real and valid significance. It highlighted the dual aspects of my nature — the active, outgoing everyday self, and the introspective aspirant. My own failings and inadequacies in the latter department, constantly emphasised by my mother, did not indicate that I could be of any use to others; but I accepted ultimately that I could at least serve as a connecting link between persons and streams of thought that might not otherwise come together.

We commenced inconspicuously. Joan, Margaret, Lois, Mrs. C. and myself were present at the first meeting, and I was in an agony of nervous anticipation beforehand as I would have to inaugurate our efforts and also 'break the ice' between strangers; but Joan and Margaret took to each other immediately, and the atmosphere warmed at once. I stressed that this was a democratic group, a mutual effort, and that we should take it in turns to direct the meeting as each thought best. This was soon shelved, however, and after several weeks they passed all arrangements to me.

After the third week Mrs. C. dropped out, I'm not sure why, as it was too early then to see how things were moving, but the following week Rose joined us, bringing with her a young medium from the Spiritualist Church named Betty, so for many weeks there were six of us. Later, Rose too, left and started an independent group of her own, and the remaining five, with occasional additions (Betty's husband was one of them) worked on together for fourteen months, regrouping further on with several persons as yet unknown to me. We were all very different in background and lifestyle, and eventually comprised Anglicans, Theosophists, Spiritualists, a Buddhist sympathiser and a Unitarian, and our ages ranged from thirty-one to sixty.

Week by week I registered a format which 'descended' into my mind, and appeared designed to encourage and promote the study and understanding of certain facets of psychological and psychical development. Set work was given, differing according to the needs of the individual, myself included — to be dwelt on during the week, written down, and eventually read out at the next meeting. We learned to meditate, to sit in silence, and to pray together, gradually attuning to each other's vibrations, and to respond by degrees to a central core of directive of which each in time became aware.

A significant aspect of the work outlined to me was a series of experiments in mental telepathy, the results of which confirmed in everyone's mind the mechanism and validity of various types of transmission. Daily, in our own homes we undertook at set times these exercises in projection and reception, and later, visual impartation of colour and symbol, followed by the generation of qualities. As the work progressed it was so arranged that those 'receiving' did not know who their transmitters were, or the nature of what was to be transmitted (whether verbal, visual, or a quality). Later still, even the time of transmission was withheld, and the identity of the transmitter was required as well.

Many results were striking and we kept meticulous records of all that transpired, including minutes of each meeting written up by members in rotation. These events of course covered many months, throughout which my life continued much as before.

Six weeks after we moved into No. 47, and all was in order — as I walked one afternoon past Patrick's site further along the road, I had the sudden, inexplicable certitude that soon we should live there. This was absurd, as the prospective owner was about to sign his contract, and was most anxious to have completion on time. But several days later the client withdrew through unforseen financial difficulties, and Patrick, deeply alarmed, tried fruitlessly for an immediate resale. When this did not materialise, our house, as always, was placed for sale as well — at a higher figure naturally than we had given for it, though not as much as I felt it was worth.

The decorations were lovely, and others thought so too, for it sold immediately and to people who wanted it straight away.

Inevitably we had to leave, and early in January moved again in much discomfort to an unfinished house without floortiles, door frames, decorations etc., etc... and once more our garden was rough fieldgrass and builder's rubble.

I tried to bear this stoically but it was hard, and to pass that immaculate garden caused me many a pang. Despite my co-operative behaviour Patrick did not approve the group meetings, though there was only one each week, attended solely by ladies who invariably left before 10.30. Every Tuesday he would act as if he had never heard of it before and express displeasure — and if he had to wait a few minutes for his cooked supper through some-one hanging on to talk, he would sulk off to bed without it and maintain a sullen silence when I tried to talk him out of it. This cast a sad blight at the end of an otherwise productive evening, and always my stomach would sink before he came home, fearful of his mood. Apart from this, things were better between us than formerly, for there was less financial strain, and the children were no longer tiny and demanding.

My mother too, expressed strong misgivings about the group, considering I was "unready" for such an undertaking, and remarking on one destructive occasion that it should be passed to Margaret's charge, she being the "most Christian" of us all (meaning the most orthodox). Margaret herself was appalled by the idea.

Why Mother felt this need to constantly criticise whatever I did, I found hard to understand. Her life was much easier than my own and more fulfilling in every way. Her healing group was large and well-attended, and she was much in demand to give counsel and contact healing to others in their own homes. She also took services at local Churches. It seemed she resented the fact that I did not regard myself as her pupil — it was impossible for me to join her group anyway, as I still could not get out at night — and perhaps another factor was that my methods and presentation were quite different to her own. I did not use her work in any sense as a prototype, though this was not deliberate on my part. Her needless hostility spoilt our relationship, and raised queries in many minds, notably Mrs. C.'s, as to my suitability as a 'teacher' (which I did not claim to be); but it was felt that a person of Mother's known spiritual stature would not criticise so strongly without cause. This sowed seeds of mental conflict and doubt even where such doubt had no foundation, and proved a foretaste in embryo of what I could expect.

During this period I received much personal interior instruction, and would waken in the night, or in the early hours of the morning, with a deep sense of awareness. Abstractions were filtered into my brain, and would emerge gradually to the forefront of my mind. I was conscious of having received tuition on some profundity by vibration, or, as I can best explain it, an inflow of white light into the frontal region of the head — this was so potent and highly concentrated it frequently took days to resolve into tangible information — even then, the substance imparted was not verifiable in any form, although I knew beyond any shadow of doubt that it was all correct. At other times there was no potency or vibration, just an experiencing which was 'knowing', deeper and more real than the most acute perception.

The knowledge ingested is almost impossible to place into words — it dealt largely with intangibilities such as the nature of sound, vibration, colour, and the illusory universe; I 'experienced' prototypes and patterns of events as they 'descended' into manifestation, and perceived in an interior sense, without visual or auditory form, how perfectly and purposefully all things were calculated and brought into expression. There are no words in our vocabulary to explain these matters — our words express structure, thought and emotion; even their finest and most ethereal connotations imply a gossamer form or essence, whereas all the spiritual perceptions referred to were beyond form in some inexplicable way — and because they were beyond form and thus beyond the illusory nature of things, they were Real, more real than anything one could conceive in one's mind. I was shown the origin of nuclear power, which lies outside the world of substances, and renders all scientific conception hypothetical. I was taught concerning the nucleus of a soul, perceiving the formative point from which it apparently emerged as a separate unit — this too, being an illusion, as the soul is at all times one with all other souls, and one with God.

One morning as I awoke, before connecting with the personality self, I experienced my identity as an infinitesimal point, like an all-seeing eye, stationed in a triangle in the apex of my head — the Universal mindstream flowing beneath its poised serenity... cluttered with all the chaotic refuse generated by the mass of unevolved mankind. Yet this also was an illusion. The finest veil lay between the Real and the unreal, casting formless Reality into perceptive symbology in the brain's effort to translate and interpret the untranslatable.

The foregoing may give a false impression with regard to my efforts in running the group. My states of heightened consciousness were fleeting and spasmodic; I had to struggle for illumination, and prayed deeply and constantly to be shown the way. There were hours spent in intense absorption and concentration, whilst my hands busied themselves automatically with some household task, or my feet walked, like an obedient horse, to the local shops.

In dreams the enlightenment continued, and circumstances affecting other people were clearly indicated. The dreams from this level contained insights into subtleties not observable in the surface personality, connected largely with accumulations of karma, or with psychological aberrations caused by conditioning. In whatever I saw, I was never permitted to feel the least criticism or superiority, for every disharmony or conflict observed in others had already been witnessed to some degree in myself.

One such perception occurred early one evening in the waking state, when I saw projected outwardly a series of harps with chords of differing colours and degrees of flexibility. One by one the harps were held before me, enabling me to discern the variations in their chordal arrangements and what these signified. There were twelve altogether, including several representing persons I did not then know. It was a strangely moving experience, and faded quickly.

On January 25th, in the midst of all the upheaval of our move into unfinished surroundings, an illumination of unusual intensity produced an extraordinary shock in my consciousness. It commenced during the moments of relaxed stillness normally preceding sleep. My mind was empty, then suddenly I entered another dimension. My physical body was *awake* — yet I stood above it in a radiant female form, knowing I was 'I', a Being unified and complete, part of a perfect, unified Whole. I knew *Myself*, my own Identity — this is very difficult to express — and the bliss of the experience was beyond description. I *knew* the world was a dream, a mirage, an illusion — brought into being solely that souls might gain consciousness; and the enormous relief of it was beyond words. With me, was He whom my soul loved; my Master, formerly encountered only in sleep. His face shone like the sun, and His whole Being exuded the most beautiful light.

He wore a white robe, as I did myself, and in His hand was a rod, like a wand, with which He touched the ethers and made them open — and I saw world upon world, layer upon layer, all interpenetrating and interlinked in the same space. Every stratum of existence was there, from the lowest grossest form, to the utterly formless — yet they were one perfect Whole, and all worlds were in reality One.

I saw my past, the long, winding path of former incarnations, co-existent with the present and the future, remembering, in the flesh, why I had been born, and that I had laboured long and arduously for what was to come. The Master was my Teacher, and I a pupil, a student in training — dedicated and intent. All that had happened to me in this life was revealed in a different context, and I saw it as I had never done before. I looked *through* the spheres *into* my physical body, knowing it to be but the instrument of the Self. The Master touched the top of my head with His rod, and golden light poured into me, stimulating and vitalising the physical organism like a charge of electricity. There was a peculiar stretching sensation in the top of my head, as if some fine and delicate membrane were manipulated and expanded — this brought the entire experience into my outer consciousness.

It all seemed to have happened simultaneously, in a timeless dimension non-existent in earthly life. As the full impact penetrated my brain, air rushed into my lungs and I re-entered my normal awareness, struggling to grasp and retain the sense of 'I' — but it slipped from me, and only the words "Of course! F.C.!" remained. Unfortunately I had no memory of what they meant. This experience had a profound effect upon me — not so much at the time, for it was so charged with light its import could not at once be grasped; but over a period of months and years, the information absorbed emerged gradually into my mental awareness.

A fortnight afterwards I picked at random from a booklist a volume by A.E. Powell called 'The Causal Body'. When it arrived and I glanced through its pages, the letters F.C. at once caught my attention. They referred to a Masonic degree. This was my first encounter with the subject, and I learned later from the work of W.L. Wilmshurst its accurate reflection, as a system, of the states and stages of a finer mode of evolutionary development.

Although this experience was clearly registered and recalled, its details were lost to me. Like most other information from this level, it was covered over in my mind and I could not use it consciously. I remembered perceiving my former lifespans but could not bring them into my memory. I had known exactly my life's purpose, and that it constituted a culmination of past effort, and would include some kind of test, or trial, or examination, the substance of which I could not retain. Only much later did I realise the inevitability of this. I could keep nothing of the past to give me courage or confidence, but must stand, at that last gate to which I came, stripped to the core, and acting from my innermost essence alone. This 'trial by fire' lay far, far into the future,* and was preceded by a stringent preparation and the traditional test — I had no idea at all, in January 1960, either of its existence, or of its nature.

There was another consequence to the stimulus given, which soon emerged with increasing strength. I became aware intermittently that I was using a new faculty, a 'seeing without sight' more real than any psychic vision, that operated quite naturally in the midst of daily life — a formless perception carrying with it an unshakable certainty.

Before this manifested, at the end of January I had a strange dream — I saw Patrick's elder brother, George, lying on the floor of an upper room, apparently dead, and as I approached him my denture fell to the bare floorboards with a clatter. I wore at that time a small dental plate holding three teeth, and it had in fact never fallen out. The dream concluded with a snow-wolf baying in the street. It made no sense to me at all, and I soon forgot it.

Late in April I took the children to tea with Rose's family. By now she had left the group, but we were good friends and met occasionally to exchange news and viewpoints. As we stood at the bus stop prior to returning home, David said something that caused me to laugh, and as I did so, to my embarrassed astonishment my denture fell out and landed in a puddle. It was then I remembered my dream.

During the ensuing week an odd phenomenon occurred. Looking out of the kitchen window when washing dishes, I saw a huge blackbird seated on the new trellis fence immediately opposite, staring directly at me. Never had I seen a bird of such

*1976/1977

size before and it made me feel uneasy. Fixedly it gazed at me, and after some minutes, flapped its great wings and flew away. Disconcerted, I recognised inwardly it was an omen of death, but pushed it from my mind.

At lunchtime, having finished a cup of tea I happened to glance idly into the cup, and was shocked to see outlined against its plain whiteness the head of a white wolf, as clearly and delicately etched as if it had been painted on the bottom. I registered the shock in my solar plexus but said nothing to Patrick who was present at the time. Two days later a telegram arrived to say George had died suddenly, and Patrick was quite stunned by it.

Within less than a fortnight the giant blackbird appeared again on the trellis, and I looked at it calmly, regarding it as proof of my own association of ideas and a certain superstitiousness. It stared as before, and then flew away.

However, to allay the sneaking doubt in my mind, I peered swiftly into my cup at lunchtime, and saw with relief its pristine whiteness, but as I put it down the light glinted on the bottom surface, and again the white wolf appeared for an instant, as clearly as if it had been painted there. Considerably shaken, I tried once more to push it from my mind. That night, shortly after falling asleep I woke abruptly, and saw poised above Patrick's head a delicately coloured arm, obviously masculine, and bent protectively. In the palm of its hand nestled a very small child, fast asleep. For a few seconds the arm remained, then slowly faded away.

I slept, vaguely comforted, and in the early hours woke again, to see, clairvoyantly this time, a hand curved tenderly round a timid mouse who peered at me from its place of safety. By second post that day came news that Patrick's little nephew had died suddenly from pneumonia — a second blow to him that sent him reeling with shock. This saddening event occurred at the time I had seen the bird. I later told Patrick of my benevolent vision, and for once was able to communicate to him something of my inner conviction, and brought him solace.

Only twice had I seen the little boy on our rare holiday visits to Yorkshire, and when I first held him, at the age of twelve months, I had known he would be difficult to rear, and feared for his parents, for his aura was very delicate and sparse.

When eventually I met the Teacher to whom these pages are dedicated*, and it was made plain to the then existing group that

*Book II, 'Beloved Executioner'.

psychism is not a desirable attribute, and best ignored — I asked why I had been given so many psychic experiences, referring specifically to this one in its several forms. He replied briefly and enigmatically that sometimes these are specially introduced into an aspirant's life as part of their training — and swiftly turned the conversation into other channels.

Reverting back to early springtime, I dreamt one night that Patrick and myself inspected a house in Canterbury Street and decided to live there. It was a lovely house and stood in sunshine, but at the dream's end I saw through an upper window the black sea observed before, lapping quietly on the furthermost boundaryline. Anxiously I turned to our Companion who had suddenly appeared — but he assured me cheerfully that the sea could not encrouch, and the house was safe.

A large, Swedish-style dwelling stood in sight of the rear of our own, in St. Alban's Road. It was unfinished, virtually a shell, and had stood this way for so long that Patrick asked me one morning to make enquiries about it, which I did. The owner for personal reasons could not complete it, and was willing to sell the house at an eventually agreed sum, and Patrick bought it.

I realised almost at once that as St. Alban's and Canterbury were synonymous in my mind as very old Cathedral cities, this could well indicate that here was our next abode. The possibility however was emphatically denied. It was "far too expensive" a house for us to live in, I was informed, and intended solely for sale. But the usual things happened, and in July we again moved, this time to 11, St. Alban's Road.

All these moves served certain purposes. Financially, they made it possible for Patrick's business to continue, and to expand, without him having a nervous breakdown with worry; and the exigences in my own life created by this means caused me to develop resourcefulness, efficiency and independence of action — also stamina and initiative. Within the circumscribed limits of my purdah-like existence I had a varied experience not possible in any other manner. And spiritually, through the dreams and intuitions that charted our course, I learned to sieve and weigh, sense and assess — deduce by 'flavour' or 'texture' the level from which the infiltrated information stemmed.

There were facets from other areas of my life likewise fully 'documented' in advance. Looking back I can see that these continued perceptions hammered into me the certitude of beneficient guidance, and compelled me to observe carefully to which aspect of my being they belonged, in order to prevent errors of judgement, as not all were precognitive. Dreams, for instance, sprang from different sources — some were simply offshoots of daily stresses; some were psychological, and however lucid, conveyed only my own slant on events and how they affected *me* as a personality. A finer stratum was more objective and was concerned with the wellbeing of others; and beyond this lay the subjective experience of the evolving self. The events awaiting manifestation from this level appeared structured solely to promote an interior growth, or alignment, regardless of the discomforts or trials these heaped upon the personality — which, strangely, despite foreknowledge, made no attempt to avoid them.

Similar equations existed in the realm of clairvoyance and clairaudience. I perceived that the entire range could be tabulated, analysed, and defined, and that its processes were as logical and orderly as our bodily mechanism.

From the time we moved, the groupmeetings were transferred to Lois's flat — as here there was no fear of interruption, and in my own home we frequently had viewers, the house still remaining for sale. In June we had reached a peak of co-operative unity, a seemingly solid achievement; and then, without warning the impetus waned — and with the onset of July, Betty, Margaret and Joan became suddenly immersed in their personal affairs, and work, meetings, and unity were abruptly abandoned.

What made it seem worse was that we now met in the afternoons, a much easier time for everyone to manage, and had made this arrangement several months previously to ensure ease of attendance. Feeling quite shocked I observed the reasons for this sudden turn of events, most of which seemed to me trivial and misplaced. Past efforts were overthrown for the most mundane of considerations, which arose like a flock of birds in our individual lives. Commitments large and small were brought into focus, demanding attention all at once, as if we must sift for ourselves what held a genuine life- importance and must be accepted, and what was merely the product and outcome of past conditioning and convention. The latter, to my amazement, with most of them came first, and caused me to wonder how much, if anything, we had learned at all, except in theory.

Lois became very critical, but I felt emotionally upset. We suspended the meetings for several weeks, and I realised for the first time that not everyone had been as absorbed as myself, much as it had meant to them.

I discovered that Theosophical meetings were held every Thursday, and feeling restless, twice prevailed upon Patrick to remain at home until 9.30 so that I could attend them and arrive back at that time.

The meetings themselves did not appeal to me, but the secretary, named Alison, who was seven years older than myself, became a close friend and joined with us in the work of the later groups. I had gone apparently on impulse, queried even by Lois — yet meeting Alison and in that particular setting turned out to be a factor of considerable consequence.

The St. Alban's Road house proved difficult to sell; in those days people tended to be wary of continental-type dwellings with their open-tread staircases, interior glass walls and wrought-iron bannisters — and we thus managed to live there for a full fourteen months before a sale was arranged. During this time my life was much fuller than formerly. It was a positive period in many ways as I learned a great deal on all levels. I also met with opposition and antagonism other than from my mother; and through my contact with Spiritualists and their Church, had to discern fast the varying aspects of my own psychology, and the psychologies of persons quite different temperamentally to myself, which was a very necessary development.

In September the group set to work again with suddenly renewed vigour, and I ought to have been happy; but something pulled at my mind which I could not locate and I lost my former sense of satisfaction. Patrick had previously begun to talk of leaving Cambridge and taking us to live in Middlesbrough, a prospect which filled me with distress. I had been there three times since David's birth (Patrick went every year), these occasions being the only holidays of that lengthy period, and remembered chiefly as times spent waiting for Patrick to return from his pubs.

I did not wish to leave Cambridge, but his assertion that he had spent all these years here for *me*, and now it was my turn to live in *his* hometown, was quite unargueable. He went off by himself to judge its feasibility, then shelved the idea temporarily (to my relief) as he wasn't too confident of the work situation. He said he would try again later.

I thought it was this that unsettled me, coupled with my earlier disillusionment, yet I had around now a number of vivid dreams which clearly portrayed group involvements and should have thus reassured me. Instead, their contents left me feeling confused, for I could not relate them to forseeable situations. I was affected by the more perplexing ones, such as walking with a large group of people through a dismal no-man's-land, holding a huge upright sword and praying constantly for protection from the adverse forces that beset us. Or acting again as midwife and holding a newly delivered infant in my arms — a factor of itself joyful — but the babies of my earlier dreams were all girls, and this was a boy, and it troubled me.

Another dream carried with it a potent vibration I learned to recognise in the future; in it I crossed a meadow, spanning a stream with my feet, and a young man approached me, weeping, and knelt like a child with his arms about me, his left hand curved in a symbolic gesture and placed against my heart. There was a feeling of deep grief and emotion; I longed to help him, but there seemed an impediment I could not undo...

Whatever the hidden reason I felt increasingly disturbed. Then unexpectedly, without any premeditation I found myself passing the group to Joan one afternoon, and asking her to allocate work and direct its procedure just as I had done, making such alteration in format as she thought necessary.

In my own aftermath of perplexity, it consoled me to recall a sleep experience I had dismissed as incomprehensible — in which Joan took us all to her home and gave each one of us new shoes to wear — very sturdy and practical; whilst at the same time I wondered at the smallness of the room in which we sat, knowing she had a large and well-lit attic-room upstairs.

Joan worked wholeheartedly and with obvious pleasure, and the others acquiesced without demur to her leadership. But she quickly dispensed with meditation and any written work of a mystical nature, running the group on a completely down-to-earth basis. It created a good, if astringent atmosphere, not unlike a convent, but as I soon felt rather a fish out of water and had said all that I apparently had to say, I quietly left, and they continued without me.

My own action vexed me with its contrariness, for I missed them all terribly — yet I felt it had been right though I could not see the reason. I became very lonely — belonging no-where, and with no-one, and a vague, wispy longing commenced deep inside me which I much later connected with my externalising linkage with the Master. The restlessness increased and I was driven by a curious urgency, so much so that one evening, on a powerful impulse, I acted against all my formerly conceived judgements — cajoling Patrick into staying in a little later than usual, and attending the healing service at the Spiritualist Church — not to receive healing, but simply to observe what went on.

Sitting in the back of the Church, I wondered what on earth I was there for — though in truth it was restful, and the prevailing tone was reverent and restrained. It was the first time I had attended a service of healing, having in fact only visited the Church a few times anyway, and always on a Sunday. The hall was dimly lit, but the medium in charge of the proceedings approached me soon after her address, recognising me as the daughter of Mrs. S., and we talked for a while. She held a group on Mondays at her home which my mother had once attended, and I now found myself asking if I might participate. She agreed at once, and I left feeling rather dazed, as I'd had no prior intention of joining any group, least of all a spiritualist one — but oddly, the restlessness had gone.

In time I realised that I was then responding to subliminal impressions — acts already designated and accepted from another level of my consciousness which my daily self had not as yet caught up with. This may have been through a lack of correct attunement of the physical vehicle, or, conversely, a deliberate movement in the dark, perhaps more effective in its untutored state for that time and place and situation.

For six weeks I went regularly to Shelford, and was greeted warmly and with friendship by the resident 'sitters'. The meetings were well-run, and the medium sincere. Seating arrangements were specified, and I was placed next to a young man named Peter, six years my junior, and soon deduced that he was the reason for my inadvertent attendance. I did not then grasp that there was another one, of a different significance, which emerged some months later.

It was surprising how much information could be imparted during odd minutes of conversation, and before long I learned of Peter's background of spontaneous clairvoyance, and of his marriage and prospective fatherhood. His psychic receptivity, in those days, was like the reflective surface of a limpid pool, and he was the most sensitive clairvoyant I had yet encountered. It astonished me that a male could be like this — I had not met with such aspiration and passivity in a man before. Another thing that astounded me was that those present, who were all good psychics, apparently had no awareness of his state (which of course he did not voice) but he was anguished inwardly, I knew, and something beyond doubt troubled him deeply.

On the sixth evening of my attendance, before the meeting commenced, I listened with a feeling akin to horror as D., an older woman, recounted the exercises she was doing with a Rosicrucian organisation, and the eerie effects they produced — which did not deter her at all. I had felt rather wary of D. all along, as she tended to 'go off' into motionless trances in which she just wasn't there, but had deflected my attention to Peter to avert the unease this created. I could not however divert my attention now, for suddenly he mentioned that he too, had joined this organisation and would soon arrive at these particular exercises himself. My blood ran cold, and I remembered spontaneously and vividly my experiences at '31' and all that they signified. I left with the strong awareness that I must not 'sit' with D.'s trances again, yet felt deeply I would be seeing Peter as I had loaned him some books and he was sure to return them. I must then talk to him seriously of the risks he took.

That night I had a terrifying dream in which I grappled with a hostile force that sought to reach him. The battle was so real I woke with a start, damp with perspiration and feeling sick — my heart thudding still with fright. But that which moved through me had beaten back the objectified entity, absorbing the impact of its ferocious onslaught; compelling it to waver and retreat.

He called at Sunday lunchtime quite unexpectedly and brought back my books. As Patrick was out, I asked him into the sittingroom and we talked unaffectedly. I told him of the alarm I had felt on hearing of D.'s experiences — from which she might hopefully emerge unscathed as she was not an ultra-sensitive type. But in my view, for what it was worth, his own receptivity was such that he ought to take very great care — and I pointed out the dangers briefly without mentioning that dreadful night. He said he would think it over, and I hoped he took me seriously. (He did not, in fact, continue further with the exercises as I learned later, but this may have been for other reasons, lack of time being one of them.)

My mother had thawed considerably towards me during the period of my visits to Shelford, considering my connection with Spiritualism a step in the right direction. Also, early in November Margaret had come to see me with a message from the group, asking me to return to them and resume its leadership. This touched me very much, for they had produced their usual amount of written work under Joan's tutelage and had managed very well in my absence. I accepted their request and started afresh; and on concluding my Shelford visits soon afterwards, rather surprisingly my mother, Rose, Lois and myself commenced a second group, for weekly meditation. This was held at my home in the evening, house-viewers having thinned out and now being almost non-existent.

At our first meeting, by Mother's wish we had asked along a well-known local medium, Mrs. B., to confirm and enlarge on whatever was operative at the time. This she did admirably but at such length that we had little time for anything else. Her main theme concerned the presence of an impulse from "a central source of Truth" that was drawing to itself a largish group of persons, ourselves included, in a context that would later be revealed.

The second meeting, without the medium this time, went equally well, and we blended harmoniously. It took the form of prayer and a visually guided meditation, with silent contemplation to conclude.

A few nights later a powerfully disruptive dream caused me much consternation. My mother approached me bearing a gift from a doctor, a jacket of white swansdown which I tried on immediately. Almost at once it tightened like a stricture, making me gasp and struggle for breath. I tried to pull it off and cried out to Mother to help me, but she remained passively seated and said it was no concern of hers. At last I tore the wretched thing from me and flung it away — at the same time glancing in a mirror, where I saw with shock that my head was completely bald. I stood then with my mother on the edge of the Estate, looking upwards at brilliant sunshine overhead. Suddenly from across the boundary line the sunlight dimmed and storm clouds scudded thickly towards the demarcation point, so that the sky above us was weirdly divided into light and darkness which reflected on the boundary marked below. Against the lurid sky appeared the figure of a Yogi beating a drum in agitated warning, and swiftly my mother turned away from me and crossed the boundaryline into the dark.

Our third meeting commenced with warm unity, and I entered the meditation with a soaring sensation, like a bird on the wing, my consciousness expanding to a state of blissful serenity and focussed seemingly in the top of my head. It was easy and effortless, totally one-pointed, and had no discernment of anything outside itself.

Mother began to speak; she gave a prayer, and then described what she saw. I cannot remember now the substance but it was quite beautifully expressed and enhanced the general atmosphere. She paused for a moment and Rose took up her theme and likewise expressed her perceptions — including the detailing of scenes from a past life in a monastic setting, shared by us all. She conveyed a deepening sense of pinpointing a specific time and circumstance, uncovering amidst the aspirational peace an increasingly serious rift between my mother and myself — at which juncture, said Rose decisively, she began to persecute me in earnest, and here it was our differences began.

While she was speaking I became aware of pictures forming in my head as if thrown up on a central screen; not the usual fleeting clairvoyance, but more solid and having a greater impact. I watched vaguely at first, merely registering them without attempting to understand their meaning. Then I remember my attention being *pulled* almost, to the symbol itself, and with increasing surprise grasped that I was *registering* vibrations in the room in symbolic form, observing passively their reflections from an impersonal height still tranquilly absorbed in light. Initially there was a rudder held in firm hands, and a lighted candle burning steadily with a lustrous flame.

At Rose's words relating to persecution, the vibrations dropped sharply — yet still I watched, without understanding — my head in the clouds. I saw a very tall tree, and a small, plated creature, like an armadillo, beginning to climb down from its lofty foliage, gradually, step by step. Suddenly it shot to the bottom, and jumped, ferociously, on a bobbing red object at the tree's foot — I had a fleeting view of the rudder, now whirling wildly out of control, and an eddy of vibration in the centre of the room rose up and hit me forcibly in the solar plexus. Harshly my mother's voice penetrated my mind, breaking up the meditation and the meeting. This was no good, she said, this was not what she wanted. Rose was "under the influence" of an unpleasant entity.

I came to myself with a jolt. My hands were gripping my stomach and for a few wretched minutes I thought I would faint — it was as if I had received a sharp electric shock. When I could speak I said to Mother, "You know you ought *never* to break up a meditation like that." but she was unmoved and unrepentant. Rose sat coldly and calmly as if nothing had happened, and only Lois expressed concern. I asked Rose to close the meeting with a prayer and then we dispersed, politely, without further discussion. I was glad to see them go, feeling shaky and ill, and was so pale that even Patrick commented on it when he came in later, a most rare occurrence and a measure of my condition. It taught me psychically a painful lesson, and I have never been so 'raw' and open since.

This finished the new group of course, but I knew I could not let it pass without comment, as Mother speedily told all our mutual acquaintances (including Joan, Margaret and Betty who had recently joined her prayer groups) that Rose had been channelling a hostile influence and was boosting her own ego. Whatever the rights and wrongs of Rose's perceptions, I did not feel that any influences had been there save human ones; and because of the implications groupwise I wrote to Mother, carefully expressing my surprise that she should flaunt the elementary rules of group meditation that she herself had taught, and describing the unfortunate consequence, so far ignored, to myself. Also my view that Rose's insights, correct or otherwise, should have been given the same hearing and courtesy as those of any other aspirant in such a group, with comments or criticisms made later at the meetings end.

This letter was unanswered, but within days she had purchased a framed inscription of Kipling's 'If' and placed it in her healing sanctuary, and Joan and Betty were tossed hither and thither emotionally, unsure whom to believe or whose account was unbiased and therefore truthful. So great was the disruption, and so widely discussed, that Joan soon produced signs of her former neurosis. I eventually resolved the crisis by contacting each of them, including Margaret, and saying they should not try to divide their loyalties but should attend either Mother's prayer group or our study group, not both while their minds were in conflict; and if they decided on the former, I would understand. Their decisions, already forseen, saddened but did not surprise me. Joan and Margaret stayed with Mother, for she "needed them most". Betty was uncertain and vacillated, then withdrew also. Lois alone stood firm. Rose, who had crossed swords with Mother before, went back to her own affairs.

Ironically, this battle for power in miniature between Rose and my mother yielded increase in attention and 'followers' for both, and myself, in the middle, was left with nothing. I immersed myself in further study, and despite the hurt at the obvious lack of confidence in my integrity, derived unexpected solace in other forms. I had by this time begun to grasp that everything has its own cycle of time and usefulness and is not intended to exceed this, however brief that cycle may be; but I did not then understand the purpose underlying the many small efforts which apparently failed or folded up on me. Later events on close study showed clearly that at each point of presumed failure, a seed had been sown that in due time was harvested, and the harvest was seldom mine alone.

During this period, my receptive mechanism produced an experience in which I saw Gurdjieff, and witnessed his System at work within me. The internal functioning of human psychology was revealed in an unexplainable way; I saw *inside* myself, and observed my own inner workings, including the intricate mechanism of thought. In states of extended awareness everything is made crystal clear and questions are no longer necessary. One realises to the full the extreme poverty and limitation of intellectual understanding, for it is impossible to describe adequately a state of consciousness outside the scope of normal experience, as the intellect is transcended at such times.

Early in January I heard that my mother had formed a new group that met in a friend's house and was concerned with the use of a ouija board. This really astounded me, as mother had always rigorously (and rightly in my view) denounced their use. I wondered what could have caused her to do this, and concluded her contacts required tangible proofs of unseen guides. Further information confirmed this, for the results had been so successful that all cautious comment was abandoned by those involved. I learned, too, that Margaret and Joan were not happy with this turn of events, it not being in keeping with the prayerful austerity which Mother normally adhered to.

Several weeks later, news reached me by the same route that the group had been suddenly disbanded, for extremely hostile and defamatory messages had begun to persistently 'come through' with my mother as their target.

I realised how humiliating this leaking information, which had gone around a bit before reaching myself, must be to her; and resolved to see her in her more chastened mood, allowing an interval to first elapse and let things cool. Feeling strongly impelled one morning I called on her and behaved as if nothing had gone amiss between us. She regarded me initially with suspicion, but soon saw that I had not come unkindly. We talked a little, and gradually she relaxed and began to tell me, almost despite herself, what had happened and how distressing it had been.

Soon I became aware of a loving Presence, and the same wave of Angelic blessing that had once poured through me instrumentally to Patrick, manifested again, to my mother — but this time it was recognised. She registered it, and her eyes filled with tears, and her brittle shell of pride and righteousness crumbled away. As I left she clung to me, and in that attuned moment I knew beyond doubt that whatever the future held, the inner bond between us could not be destroyed and I would love her always.

During the winter Patrick woke me one night in a state of shocked distress, and at length admitted he had had a dream which upset him deeply. He was sure I had died, for he searched for me everywhere, grieving terribly, yet could not find me. I comforted him by saying I did not believe I was destined to die yet awhile as there were too many indications of activity ahead. He accepted this, and as the impact soon faded from his mind, appeared to forget the dream altogether, and certainly did not refer to it again.

Relating to this, though I did not then know it, were several dreams of my own. Twice I woke in the night crying audibly, "No, no, no!" having dreamt the house was on fire and Patrick trapped in it. Each time I saw him dragged clear, but feared he was badly burned and woke before I could find out. In another dream he shouted angrily at me, accusing me violently and unjustly of things I could not recall — though I knew I had not merited his aggression. As he shouted the ground between us was split by an earthquake, leaving him on one side of the rift and myself and the children on the other. Both children were shocked and crying — but there were no indications of what this was about. My only clue, if one could call it such, came from a further dream in which we sat in his van, with Patrick swearing and raging because it would not go — the sides, he insisted, were collapsing and falling to bits... whereas from my vantage point beside him the van was in perfect order, and moving very fast along the main road to the city centre.

In February Joan visited me and renewed our friendship, soon followed by Margaret, then Betty. In this month too, was brought together a new group consisting of four women, all very recently bereaved, whom I had met over the years and now recontacted in daily life on the estate. I invited Betty to demonstrate psychometry for them, which she did very sensitively, and we talked over their queries and I think they found some comfort. All had young children, and a measles epidemic soon concluded the arrangement, but not before each person concerned had read several books and absorbed fresh insights.

A second venture commenced in March on similar lines to the original study group, having three of its members — Joan, Betty and Lois, and the addition of Peter, who said he would come when he could. Margaret was temporarily not with us through Church and other involvements; but Rose, whose own group had again foundered, came in her stead. This project showed every evidence of success and was swiftly followed by the formation of a third group, quite different in type, and comprising persons not connected with before. It was more mentally orientated than the earlier meetings, requiring far greater effort on my part, for Alison, Veronica and Ann were intellectually inclined and had studied extensively. The former two were Theosophists and well versed in all aspects of the Society's doctrines, both exoteric and esoteric. Ann had a background of Theological study and was extremely intelligent and well-read. This group was difficult to stabilise on a sound basis but immensely rewarding. It provided a stimulus and an encouragement to express far more than had previously been possible. Yet here too, occurred the curious unlocking touched on formerly with Joan; and Veronica, rather brittle on the surface, confronted a crisis and plumbed her own depths in a sincere and very moving fashion.

It was Veronica also who provided an almost obligatory connection with a force-field channelled via her husband, a dedicated Lodge member, the nature of which had already been confronted when at '31'. This created an opportunity for indirect assessment, and was part of my own initial preparation for what still lay years ahead. We can only see in retrospect with what patient care we are trained, and how stage by stage we are taught to bear and offset certain currents.

This new group worked hard and attentively; and both on work levels and in our inner lives, we were again made aware of the interrelatedness of individuals and events, and the all-controlling activity of the Unseen.

Parallel with the waxing and waning of these three groups came another development, which began with a visit from Mr. K., a friend of the Shelford medium, who himself held a responsible position in the Spiritualist Church. His visit was entirely unexpected, its purpose being to ask if I would accept nomination for the Church Presidency — a proposition which left me flabbergasted, for I had only recently become a member.

I protested that I wasn't fundamentally a Spiritualist and had only attended a handful of services plus the group of which he knew — and furthermore that I could not support certain of their procedures ('open' circles to name but one). He lightly over-rode these objections and said that he and others had noted that I seemed able to get things moving, and they thought I ought to do this through the Church, which had need of persons of initiative. For this reason the small matter of my lack of proper-term membership could be quite easily overcome.

I asked for time to think about it, and eventually accepted as I felt deeply it was a proffered opportunity. Rather foolishly I thought this meant more scope and the possibility of presenting to others what was most dear to me. I can see now that whatever purposes may have been served elsewhere, for myself what came next was a kind of cramming, a process of further education, specialised and intensive — highlighting the unconscious functions of the human mind and psychology, and the way their suppressed or hidden content externalises inevitably into life.

News in such areas spreads like wildfire, and I was soon asked to take several services, both in the Church of my nomination and the National Spiritualist Church in the city. I insisted I could not give the customary clairvoyance, but was asked to speak despite this. Abjectly nervous, I tried — and it wasn't too bad, though quite different to talking in a small group. On the third occasion my injunction about the clairvoyance was 'forgotten', and when already on the platform I learned that a medium had not been booked for this purpose — the Chairman precipitating me into it without any ado or consultation. Almost paralysed with nervousness I just stood still behind the rostrum wishing the floor would open and swallow me up. Then I felt a cold breeze immediately behind me and sensed vividly a young and agitated man — it seemed I could do it after all. The sensing was acute, so close and urgent that it made me gasp for breath and I had difficulty to impart the symbols that rose in my mind — these came so clearly that in one case a lady cried and said I had brought back her son. But I did not like doing this, although it was deemed a success, and for some inexplicable reason even to myself, I declined to do it again. However, my reputation as having 'the sight' was made, and in May I was elected President, inveigling the help of Rose as my deputy, for she knew all the ropes.

Mr. K. at this point decided I ought to have the makings of a healer, and being himself a recognised healer of repute, undertook to give me training and instruction. I wasn't too sure about this, never having been drawn to the 'laying on of hands' as my mother was. But I remembered my dream of the nurse ("I heal"), and duly presented myself.

My task was to assist Mr. K. with six patients, and tell him between times if I had picked up any symptoms. It soon appeared that I was the type who took into herself and reflected the symptoms of others — and by the sixth patient I was feeling pretty worn-out and exhausted. I knew nothing of their ailments or past histories, and this last person, metaphorically, almost knocked me out. She was in early middleage, and looked plumpish but rather wan. Contact with her drained me at once of all energy I had left, and suffused me utterly with a heavy, greyish-yellow matter which clogged my system with unconsciousness and a desire to sleep.

I excused myself and staggered home feeling rather alarmed, and it took over two days to regain my wellbeing, in which time I decided that contact healing was not for me, and this too I declined to afterwards participate in. Within a fortnight the sixth patient passed peacefully away with a terminal cancer, known of, naturally, to Mr. K., who had helped keep her going through operations etc. for some time. This incident, and others foregoing, gave me much food for thought about my own mechanism. It was ultra-sensitive, and had the same faculties and potential as all genuine mediums and healers, yet I could not use it as they did, nor was I intended to, and this I knew beyond any shadow of doubt. What then, was it for? But there was no answer, and I wondered rather miserably if my mother was right, and I was simply "unready".

Now came a difficulty and the second group was suddenly upturned. This came about initially through Joan's observation of my attitude towards Peter, which, as she reported to my mother, "betrayed Kate's love for him" and in her view was grossly unfair to Patrick. Her censure was unconcealed and severe, for I had committed the grave error of showing interest in a man other than my lawful spouse — this being construed as "disloyalty".

I had been deeply concerned about Peter, who needed, I felt, a more specialised assistance than that provided by the group, and my 'attitude' or attention was an attempt to redress this — though there is no doubt his gentleness and aspiration evoked in me a response. But he came only twice, having a young wife who since the birth of their baby did not like to be left, and the second occasion had precipitated Joan's assertion. My mother ought to have known better than to take it seriously, but I expect it was too good a fuel to forego and the temptation proved too strong. She required from me, in Joan's presence, a full and complete exposition of my very limited contact, and then passed the comment that a person of Joan's devout integrity would not create so very much smoke without fire. This comment of course went the rounds, and my attempt at compliance thus had the reverse effect of the one intended. Betty and Lois both said that Joan was being foolish, but the damage was done and doubts were again sown widely afield about my worthiness. The story spread that I had allowed myself to fall in love under the pretext of "teaching". It caused a small storm amongst the more Christian and moral of our acquaintance and considerable distress to myself. This may sound extreme but is in fact an understatement. That the same concern and attention had been given to others, and to Joan in particular, quite escaped notice. Peter was male, and this made all the difference.

Having said her piece and caused havoc, Joan withdrew from the group and said she would prefer to join the all-female one, which she did. Rose at this juncture found further willing sitters for her own concerns, and Betty also tried forming a group, which left her no time for the one in hand. Peter gave up the unequal battle against circumstance, and Lois alone remained. So she too passed to the third group, and was soon joined by Margaret; and these meetings continued constructively throughout the summer.

Perhaps this is a good place to refer to the preponderance of group formations, which proved generally disruptive and held things up time and again. Here I risk sticking my neck out and getting my head chopped off, for I must state categorically that I knew, by proven inner signals over a lengthy period, that each impetus I *consciously* acted upon from a recognised level, was designed to an end by a higher Intelligence than I could encompass. What that end was, I did not know, nor could I formulate it — but that we all moved inexorably towards a specific event was genuinely apprehended. We were drawn together to act and react upon one another, to observe our own behaviour and learn by it; to turn inwards and connect with the higher levels of our own development already existent — and to generally reorient ourselves preparatory to, and in order to benefit from, the tuition of that greater Being who called us to Him.

It seemed to me that such signals, registered as the result of prolonged training, and utilised as a means of drawing people together in working groups, were the only ones permissable — for to tap unconscious and subconscious depths in another, without proper directive, is like entering upon an uncharted sea on the darkest of nights and lacking a compass. The continual drawing in by would-be teachers, notably Rose, and later Betty, of unselected persons for unspecified purposes, could, and often did (particularly in the future) create chaos for all concerned. I have not included my mother for she always stated that she acted solely from interior guidance, and it is not my place to gainsay this — certainly her prayer and healing groups were aspirationally based and did good work. What came later was rather different and does not belong here. But in 1961 I did not voice these unpopular intimations, knowing well the tenuousness of my own hold on the attention of others at the best of times — and I had already learned that on the odd occasion when I asserted I 'knew', reactions ran high.

It is a sad fact that people do not like you if you say you 'know' something that is concealed to them, even if it is in their own best interest that you say it, and it is later proven to be correct. They choose merely to consider you suffer from an elevated opinion of yourself, and treat you accordingly.

My contact with the Spiritualist Church soon relieved me of many illusions and constituted a compression of experience into the shortest possible timespan — the process of which inevitably involving and affecting others. The Master scattered seeds amongst us willy-nilly; and in silence, and unseen, some germinated and took root, and others lay dormant for a future time.

Almost immediately I discovered that a figurehead can be hated, abused, misquoted, lied about, and deliberately inveighed against — without doing anything at all to merit it, simply because they hold a coveted office of supposed authority. In effect there was no authority at all. My committee, mainly seasoned diehards, grumbled, complained, backbit, ruthlessly criticised — and stolidly blocked virtually everything I tried to do. They had no intention of changing anything, and as a majority vote was almost impossible, nothing could be changed, and I soon wished heartily I had not become involved.

Patrick didn't think much of it all, but as it took only two evenings each week on both of which I was home by 8.30, he could not really complain, and even the monthly committee night extended the service by only one hour. All in all he had little to protest about, and still kept his sights upon moving to Middlesbrough as and when he could collect his capital together.

Shortly after my inauguration I was allowed to arrange, at my own suggestion, a ceremony of rededication for Church workers, Healers, and the Committee, which evoked a surprising atmosphere of harmonious unity and aspiration, that more than balanced the earlier unpleasantnesses. This proved the apex of my sphere of influence, and nothing later in the nine months of my sojourn as President could measure up to it. This special service was also my sole opportunity of communicating with Peter on an esoteric level.

I dreamt beforehand of my links with these new acquaintances, and perceived clairvoyantly the form the service should take. I also saw, in the strange, semi-sleep state between sleeping and waking, a North American Indian ceremony of initiation, for the coming-to-manhood of a young brave.

The service produced a profound effect upon Peter, who sought me out afterwards and tried to express how he felt. We talked in the small committee room with people coming and going — all 'lit' and friendly, and all at their most benign best. Beneath the halting efforts of articulation, impressions moved soundlessly between us. I saw that his heart was open, and heard him inwardly cry out to me — the anguished, unearthly cry of a soul stirring into wakefulness whilst still encased in the prison of materiality.

He needed desperately to talk, and even more to cry — to wash away from him the enclosing walls of solitariness, but here there was no privacy for either. Those in and out, or present, exuded goodwill, and each had aspired wholeheartedly during the preceding hour, but did not touch the chord that for a very brief while resounded within him.

In my worldly foolishness I imagined that if I was older it would have been permissable to draw him to me and help him, without the battery of insinuation and slander which I knew I would reap if I attempted it now. I let him pass by me, for I could do no other. At the moment of greatest intensity Patrick called to collect me, and I had to leave — the words unspoken, the tears unshed. But I believed in my heart I could have helped him — that the seed that fell asleep in him so quickly could have grown and flourished here and now — and grieved that through the heedless words of others this was denied.

I thought too, that the ill-will brooding so thinly beneath the surface was the impediment I had seen in my dream of the meadow. But my assumptions, on all counts, were incorrect, and far, far, from the mark.

Apart from the re-dedication service, my only happy recollection from my term as President is of the many friendships with church helpers, and the aged and infirm who attended the services of healing. Most of these people were simple and prayerful, serving their Church and their Maker with a loving integrity that gladdened one's heart; those who benefitted from the devoted work of the healers expressing their gratitude, whenever possible, in humble acts of service. I could not help but become fond of them, and their very real sincerity moved me deeply, and eased the heartaches caused by those of consequence in higher places.

At the end of July a buyer was at last found for our house, and Patrick, released potentially of its burden, determined to uproot us as speedily as possible. He knew I'd had my fill already of the joys of Presidency, and assumed I think, that to leave the trials and vexations encountered all round would not trouble me overmuch. The 'third' group still worked with enthusiasm and in harmony, and Betty had also joined after disappointments elsewhere; but I felt now, as in the previous September, that I had poured myself out to my limit and had said all I had to say, and that perhaps after all I should not resist Patrick's legitimate desire to leave Cambridge and return 'home'.

In this frame of mind I produced a most lucid dream. I stood in front of a full-length mirror and instead of seeing myself imaged in the glass, the figure of Father Joseph, robed in blue, confronted me — and holding my eyes with his own, said firmly, "You must stay *here.* There is much work for you to do." And I awoke.

The children suddenly grasped their father's intention, and raised strong and loud protests. David was in his last year at junior school and had just obtained a grammar scholarship. He had many friends on the estate, was athletic and popular, and most certainly did not wish to yield up his assets. Teresa, too, lived a full and happy life, and was much attached to my new sister-in-law, who indulged her quite shamefully and allowed her to share in all the excitements of wedding gifts and a luxurious domesticity. Both asserted they did not like Middlesbrough, and Patrick left stubbornly, feeling none too pleased with his offspring.

He came back a week later full of the newly built houses he had inspected — much cheaper than their Cambridge equivalents — and he had already selected one for us and wished me to see it. My heart sank and I didn't know what to do, but eventually, in fairness, said if he really wished to go so much then he should leave ahead of us and buy the small business he intended, also the house, and we would follow. This pleased him and off he went once more, though I felt wretchedly uncertain about what I was agreeing to, yet it seemed at the time the right thing to do.

While he was away I dreamed vividly — and saw myself climbing many stairs to a turret-like tower. The staircase spiralled endlessly, and I was crying, and heavy with pregnancy. Right at the top, in a little bare room with a nun to assist me — I gave birth to a child after very real and difficult labour, the pain so acute it was hard to believe I was dreaming. I remember saying to the nun, "It cannot be born yet, I must wait for hours...", but she replied in a firm voice, "It will be born *now* — you see!" And sure enough a beautiful child was born. I saw then a number of scrolls inscribed with diagrams and print, and was told that this was the work the child would do.

A few nights later I dreamt that a man in army uniform, perhaps dating from 1914, or maybe earlier — was conducting a search of some kind. He was moving from place to place and carrying a photograph in his hand. Before long he entered the large upper room where I sat with a number of people, and one by one he approached them, looking intently into each face, then turning away. At last he came to me, and with a cry embraced me as if I was someone dear to him. Tears streamed down his face, and he sank to his knees and placed his hand in a symbolic sign against my heart. Feeling quite stunned, I saw that the photograph he held was very old — a daguerreotype — and was of myself.

Months afterwards came another dream of this strange sign, in which I stood in the aisle of a single-decker bus next to a dark young man, rather Indian looking. He turned towards me suddenly and I felt a deep and overwhelming emotion as he made the same sign and gesture.

Patrick returned after a week in a very different frame of mind; for further investigation had revealed considerable unemployment, and this alarmed him more than anything else could do. Sternly he told me that we would have to remain in Cambridge, as if myself, or the children, would raise an objection — and turned his attention immediately to finding another house, as our contract was signed and we must soon go.

Greatly relieved, I helped him to look, and to negotiate more land; then I drew-up the plans. In sleep the area we would live in was pinpointed, and though Patrick tried to buy a house elsewhere — at virtually the twelfth hour he changed his mind and bought instead the one I had 'seen'. Thus, in September we moved to 45, Metcalfe Road, on the opposite side of the Estate, and a new phase began.

PART 3

APPROACH TO THE TEACHER

You have a duty to perform. Do anything else,
do any number of things,
occupy your time fully,
and yet, if you do not do this task,
all your time will have been wasted.

Jalaludin Rumi

Idries Shah, 'The Way of the Sufi' p. 110, Octagon Press Ltd. 1968.

Our new garden was brilliant with dahlias, and my first impression of the house and its environs was of colour and orderliness. This seemed a good sign, and like a blind idiot, I cheerfully assumed it presaged the future. But my life there was to be anything but orderly — though it was certainly colourful!

Our last month at St. Alban's Road had seen me in a ferment of activity. Not connected with the move, for I have never packed until a few days before leaving, aiming always at as little disarrangement as possible for the children's sake. My industry was concerned with a project which bored relentlessly in my mind, and ignore it as I may (and I tried hard to do so) it gave me no rest.

At last I acceded that, crazy though it seemed, I must do something concrete about it, and at this point my potent inner conviction and commensurate mental certitude dissolved into a fearful timidity. My head was full of unwritten articles and the pressing urge to organise, cohese and arrange; yet my emotions seethed restlessly like a pot on the boil. I knew I must initiate fresh work and widen my contacts, and that this held an 'X' factor which caused me to tremble inwardly, though I could not fathom why.

Having 'wrestled with the angel' to no avail, I set to work diligently to express the impetus that coursed through me, and commenced writing what eventually transpired to be a series of twelve lectures, incorporating the entire fruit of my interior experience. Around these lectures I laid out on paper a kind of framework — a structure of learning, containing in course form the titles of books in my possession which had proved the most helpful and informative to myself and others, and setting out also the meditations etc. that had been utilised throughout nearly two years of groupwork. With the intended addition of other material, I saw beyond doubt that I had the beginnings of a tutorial system.

Apprehensively I mentioned this to Joan, who was newly pregnant and very pleased about it and therefore in a receptive frame of mind. She expressed enthusiasm — for it was surely a good idea to pass on to others what had benefitted ourselves. Tentatively I mentioned the formation of a Brotherhood, a group prepared to assist and encourage lone students, by post, who might lack the opportunities and group-contact we had been given. Again she concurred, and feeling heartened, I quelled my nervousness sufficiently to write out introductory papers for this small 'event'.

It will be seen by the foregoing that however firmly grounded I was inwardly, my somewhat narrow life and the still existent suppression that I lived under, considerably affected my external personality — and I needed these cowardly 'props' to give me sufficient confidence to do what I had to do. A united venture was one thing to acquaint Patrick with, but lone initiative was quite another, and would have proved exceedingly disruptive.

There was a pause whilst we moved house, and I closed the 'third' group (now the sole group) for a fortnight, but continued with my duties as President. I tried to indraw deeply, and as I worked, sought repeatedly to ascertain the correctness of what I proposed to do. I needed time to deliberate, to delve consciously to the root of this outgoing impetus that precipitated me purposefully along the relentless uphill path I so feared to take. But there was no time. Pressurised to exhaustion in both inner and outer life, the impulse nevertheless persisted, and in mid-October the Fountain School of Philosophy came into being almost without my volition.

This of course sounds very grand, and I really thought it would involve many people, but it was not to be so. It was a structure for specific persons and specific purposes — in retrospect I can see why it had to be, and the function it served; but at that time I had only my own assumptions to work from, and these, as almost always, were misplaced.

What I tried to do belonged really to the future — yet its backward and inaccurate reflection was not an ill-timed error. By strangely intricate design it gave me my first conscious insight to a form of functional linkage then quite unknown to me, which, though actually experienced, remained dormant in meaning as so much else of consequence, until its appointed hour of understanding.

This project got off to a promising start. The group reassembled in full strength, including Rose, and discussed the idea of a

Brotherhood and agreed its formation. Even my mother deigned to be an honorary member on the strength of the first three lectures, now written, which she approved; though I suspected she regarded herself more in the capacity of a consultant. Peter — not present, but "with us in spirit" was also honorary, and only Veronica, away on holiday, remained in ignorance of all that was proposed.

So far, so good. But the School itself was another matter, and here I met a stumbling-block. Despite the interest, enthusiasm and approbation, it had to be a solo effort. When it came down later to committal, no-one was prepared to take any personal responsibility, and although on that auspicious evening they all said they would "think about it", I soon grasped that this was the way it was going to be.

Everyone dispersed in a spirit of goodwill, and I felt rather perplexed at my own flatness, as I had apparently achieved a successful beginning. And I did not really mind about the School-work, being quite happy to continue its promotion on my own — the Brotherhood background was a bulwark which would render it workable for me. Yet I went to bed in an uneasy frame of mind, and dreamt two dreams which did nothing to alleviate this. In the first I held a yellow canary perched on the palm of my hand and singing fullthroatedly. An angry blackbird swooped suddenly down and pecked it viciously, stifling at once its song. In the second I sat in a dentist's chair, and carefully, methodically, one by one he extracted four teeth, without anaesthetic. Agonised, I asked if he had finished, and he peered thoughtfully into my mouth. No, he said, there's still another to come out, but you can keep it a little bit longer.

The uneasiness persisted, but I worked with a will and produced more lectures and the introductory papers for the School, which was briefly advertised in several appropriate magazines. I managed to buy a primitive duplicator and was actually helped by Patrick to roll-off a multitude of leaflets. I think in the back of his mind he concluded I was creating a business as I had gone about things in a business-like way; and though I stressed fees would be minimal and simply to cover costs, he did not react as I had feared.

The Church work continued as before. There was Harvest Festival, which was lovely, and a fund-raising Social that also went well, but the spiritual zenith had been reached and passed;

goodwill was lukewarm, and the atmosphere increasingly mundane.

On Veronica's return, she and Alison visited me and I placed in her lap the newly duplicated introductory papers which the others had already received. She read them quietly whilst Alison and myself talked amicably. Almost at once the atmosphere in the room altered, as if it had been charged with alien currents. Veronica, no longer warm and friendly, said sharply did I realise she was a member of the T.S. Esoteric Section (I did not) and as such could have nothing whatever to do with anything like *this*. She stood up and curtly expressed what she thought of it, and the dark, obsessive force I had felt with her husband, flowed through her and struck me a seemingly forcible blow in the solar plexus. Alison's face paled, and I watched her calm certitude and staunch support suddenly waver, for she too was a longstanding member of the Theosophical Society, and had already experienced a conflict of allegiance in the past.

Dumbly, I let Veronica say what she would, and could find no words with which to answer her. It was without doubt the end of the friendship between us, which might never have existed judging by the way she looked at me. Soon they left, and feeling very shaken I collected my rejected papers from the floor and puzzled over what had provoked such a violent reaction. But I could see nothing offensive in what I had written, and was too upset to realise that the words themselves did not constitute the problem — it was the impetus behind them that people pitted themselves against.

Two meetings had been arranged for the following week, one of which was a continuation of the former group, and the second for the commencement of a series of experiments designed to assess the effects of chromotherapy as a healing agent. This latter was to take place fortnightly and was largely for Peter's benefit, for he was interested in all forms of healing and practised in the Church as a contact healer.

We had already talked about this 'laying on of hands' at some length, for he, like myself, tended to take on and retain the symptoms of others, and whereas I had withdrawn because of this, he had not, and the adverse effect was frequently obvious. I had tried cautiously to induce him to stop, and this he seemed willing to do; but Mr. K. whose star pupil he was, did not approve my advice and resented what he felt was interference. I understood this, naturally, for who was I (an "untrained psychic" as one lady put it) to make comment on such a matter? His sponsorship of myself had markedly subsided when it became clear that I would neither blossom into a platform medium, or a healer, a factor that was completely misunderstood. Peter was now a sore subject between us, no longer to be mentioned, and I knew quite well he would not be pleased when he heard about the chromotherapy.

It was now late October, and on the day arranged for our first meeting came letters and telephone calls explaining, very reasonably, why members could not come — and none did. But the chromotherapy group went well, and Peter, Lois, Betty, and a friend from the March groups who acted as 'guinea pig', had an interesting evening during which Peter clearly demonstrated his abilities and potential. The following week again brought letters and phonecalls, and groupnight, strangely, remained groupless.

On November 8th, my distressing dream of '31' at last materialised, and I answered the door in the early afternoon to a woman who urged me to come at once to the school, for my child had had an accident in the playground and they did not know how serious it was. An ambulance was already on its way to take her to hospital, and I must go too. This was the moment that every mother dreads, and terrorstricken I was driven to the school, comforted only by the memory of a recent perception in sleep of a child falling heavily on tarmac, and being afterwards conveyed by stretcher to an ambulance — knowing as I observed the scene that the child would survive unharmed. Here indeed my faith was put to the test. Teresa spent five days in hospital, and such was the nature of her injury that it was several days before we knew for certain no lasting damage was done. I thanked the Master with grateful heart. All else I could bear, I said, all else — not knowing the degrees of grief and pain, and that we have links of love that are not of the body, but can cause us equal anguish.

My mother heard of the chromotherapy and expressed great alarm. Healing was not my province, she declared. I was not equipped to 'teach' it; I had "insufficient experience", and it would be years yet before I was 'ready'. I should stick to lectures and Churchwork! If I persisted in trying to 'heal' I would reap ill-health and trouble. There was "darkness around me" already...

I protested that I wasn't teaching — we were conducting properly recorded experiments in colour transmission, nothing more. But this was construed an evasion. Either I must cease this meddling or she would rescind her honorary membership and withdraw her support from my efforts altogether. Dismayed, I tried to placate her, for I knew this would lead to the usual conflict of loyalties and cast doubts on the validity of what I was trying to initiate. My arguments were in vain. Nothing would do, it seemed, but to abandon the new group. It was, however, my only link with Peter and my sole means of reaching him. I was aware that it must not capsize as yet for some reason, so I declined to close it, and Mother at once withdrew, just as she had threatened.

Within a few days Joan visited me, looking very pregnant and not at all well. Things were not right with her physically and she seemed quite depressed and unlike her usual self. We talked for a while about recent events, and at length she said, very seriously, that she wondered if I could be mistaken in what I did, and was perhaps unwittingly "working for evil" as so many things were against me. I listened with horror — feeling stunned that she could entertain such a thought. It sounded unreal, but she meant it, and numbly I realised that she too, was moving away from me.

At this juncture the first responses to my advertisements began to arrive, and with fresh hope I sent off the introductory literature and waited expectantly — having dreamt of several people I did not yet know, but whom I felt would enter my life through the coursework. I looked forward to acquainting the others with these letters of enquiry, waiting optimistically for their arrival on the doorstep for what should have been the fourth meeting of our new arrangement. Only Margaret came; a solitary figure, tired out and apologetic. The reasons for continued absences were all valid — either personal illness or the illnesses of others. Alison, for instance, wrote me a warm and friendly letter disassociating herself from Veronica's viewpoint, but unable to join us as her sister-in-law had a terminal illness, and for the time being she was totally committed within the family. Yet valid as the reasons were, it was still most odd the way things had come to a standstill.

Around now came an experience which was very brief, but potent. Months previously I had read an article on the Great Pyramid, and had often thought of its interior structure — the ascending passages, the pit, the Queen's Chamber... and the King's Chamber at the top with its stone sarcophagus. I felt it held an equation with the Masonic Degrees, but my speculations had gone no further than this. One evening, just before falling asleep, I saw a shaven-headed priest, white-clad in a robe of Egyptian style, standing near the bedside and carefully storing a recording scroll in what looked like a cubbyhole in the wall. For some reason it caused me to think of the Pyramid, and suddenly a voice — soft, but soundless — *breathed* against my ear in silent transmission. It said, "*This* is the King's Chamber", and momentarily I was inside a pyramidal cone in the apex of my head, and I *Knew*. But what I knew I could not remember, it faded at once, and left the curious sensation of a Mystery inwardly registered, and stored for future use.

On the evening of the third Chromotherapy meeting, Peter presented himself looking drained and unwell. He tried valiantly to work as before, but it was clearly no use, and I stopped him. He admitted to pains and discomforts that he believed had been absorbed from various patients the previous evening, and again I stressed his folly as firmly as I could without giving offence. His aura was grey, and it seemed to me that the area around the solar plexus was torn, a factor I had noted before, and which made him in my view peculiarly vulnerable. I saw too, a double headed horse looking both ways at once, indicating a divided mind — or divided loyalties.

But the evening passed quite well in general discussion, though the earlier impetus had gone. When we broke up, Peter lingered behind on the doorstep. It seemed he had something more to say to me; and ironically, at his lowest ebb, and at an inopportune moment, he was ready at last to unburden himself of whatever caused him anguish. He expressed himself in troubled, hesitant phrases, and my heart ached desperately for him, for I knew with sad insight all that ailed him, and the long road home. I wished, helplessly, that I could ask him in again to talk, but Patrick was due back any minute, and I was well aware of the sheer futility of attempting private conversation with a young man, especially one in the emotional condition so apparent now in Peter.

I gave him what verbal comfort I could, and what counsel was in me. But I did not tell him what I saw, or what I knew, for it would resolve nothing for him and might even make things worse. There were structures built up in the distant past which effectively blocked his way, and could only be by-passed with the far-seeing aid of a Master. For this to be possible, certain things were necessary and must be set in motion in advance — to listen was of itself not enough. Sadly, as was soon evident, although he had listened, he did not act — and allowed himself to be led away from the proffered opportunity of contact that lay waiting, unknown to any of us as yet, less than a year off in the future.

There were no further colour experiments, for the other members of this group were confronted with personal difficulties which kept them from attending, and it was not possible for Peter to come on his own without them. He telephoned once, and later he wrote, and it seemed he had temporarily at least, discontinued the contact healing to enable his system to right itself. There were now no meetings at all; a complete full-stop... and all I had planned came to nothing.

Throughout this period I had many dreams relating to people and events, three only of which I will include here. In the first I was stabbed in the back, and registered incredulously that my attacker was Peter. In the second, Rose, her face black like a Negress, came down some stairs outside the Church committee room (where there were no stairs, in fact) and deliberately slashed my arm to the bone with a dagger, laying it bare and exposed. I stared at her in silent disbelief, then walked past her and out of the door to the street beyond. The third dream was of a different nature entirely, stemming from a deeper, more conscious stratum of my being, and I *lived* it, becoming acutely fatigued both physically and mentally in the sleep-state. The dream was as follows:-

A large gathering of people had been called together for a specific test or examination. Those participating were grouped in a circular compound surrounded by high wire fencing, and crowds of non-participants collected on the outside to watch. The test appeared to be simple. Each candidate had to run swiftly whilst remaining on the same spot. Everyone commenced with apparent confidence, though I was apprehensive and thought I had little chance of enduring for the allotted period. After a short while people began to drop out, at first in ones and twos, then in large numbers. I could feel the muscular pain in my legs and the growing exhaustion, but fixing my mind on the task in hand, kept on. In the background stood the Master, watching us all intently. Looking up a little later I was surprised to find only a small group left, and then even these fell out one by one till only three of us remained. At last the Master stopped us — the other two were exhausted and hardly moving their feet at all, but I seemed to have overcome my limitations and was strong and revitalised, knowing that I could continue indefinitely on an inner momentum. The Master appeared pleased though He made no comment. Instead He took me to look at a board where the names of the successful candidates had been prominently displayed — I clearly saw those of the two who 'passed' with me, but my own was not there. I felt bewildered, for I knew my name should have headed the list.

Early in December, two persons registered with the Fountain School as postal students, shortly followed by a third. The first was Mary, a housewife in her early fifties, the second, Vera, the young widow of a clergyman, and the third, Phillip, a schoolmaster nearing forty. These three people worked diligently, conscientiously and with enthusiasm. They were a joy to me. With their worksheets came letters and I soon felt I knew them all well — as indeed I did, for each of them had been previously contacted in sleep, and this steady stream of informative linkage continued just as it had with the former groups.

Before this could become established, we held our first Brotherhood function — a Christmas service with readings and carols, followed by cake and wine. It was held at the home of Betty and Rupert; he too, being a member.

We were eleven in number, but only six of us could be present — Betty, Rupert, Rose, Lois, Alison and myself. I brought with me two packs of tall, slim candles, twelve in all — six red and six blue; and eleven of these were lit to represent each one of us, my mother included, as her hostility had waned with the cessation of Peter's group.

It was on this occasion, the first in my life, that I was aware of an interim form of communication; the Teacher drew close to me and projected his words through my mind so that I spoke them simultaneously. I was completely conscious of this — it was a tenuous feeling, utterly passive, like resting in safe, strong arms whilst this Greater Being overshadowed me. In later years the mode was different, dynamically active and direct, and this will be mentioned in its proper place.

As I spoke to those assembled I heard of course, my own words — and realised that if my ability to translate mental impulses proved inadequate, I had certainly 'cooked my goose' — for I spoke of a Brother who would join us in the flesh towards the end of the coming year, and for whom we should light the twelfth candle as a symbol of his presence. That as a group we, and others linked to us, all approached a demarcation line in our lives and development which would manifest as an event fixed in time, and was connected with the initial impetus, or foundation, of spiritual work for the coming era. This event presented each one of us with a special opportunity, inwardly acknowledged and prepared for over a lengthy span of incarnations. Some of us however, had been held-up and had allowed ourselves to be side-tracked, and would thus find it more difficult to attain readiness (or to be there) on time and reap the inherent possibilities of this predestined situation. I cannot quote more with any accuracy — it faded quickly from my mind, though its impact long remained.

At the close of the service when the candles were extinguished, and just before putting on the lights — some curious things occurred. Peter's candle fell down, and my mother's bent in two. Rose's slid suddenly to the floor with a soft bump — and she said as this happened her stomach seemed to sink, for she knew it had a meaning. But quickly we all relaxed and put aside these omens, which might, after all, be pure chance — and were happy together. The piano was piled with our small gifts to each other and included those sent by absent friends. I heard with pleasure that Joan's husband, Ian, had also delivered letters and gifts in the afternoon.

Soon we were joined by Nigel, Alison's husband, who arrived officially to take her home but was induced to stay and share the cake and wine. He sat himself next to me, and beneath the gay babble of conversation, thanked me with seriousness for the prayers that had been offered regularly for his dying sister.

I knew Nigel slightly in a business capacity for he was one of the many Estate Agents with whom I'd had contact. Alison had told me that he jokingly (and rudely) always referred to me as 'Psychic Sue', and this change of demeanor was both surprising and oddly moving. There was no doubt at all he had suffered greatly through his sister's long and tragic illness, and as we talked I saw suddenly that his heart was open — as Joan's and Peter's had been, and a faint blue lotus, exquisitely shaped, appeared interiorly in this region of his chest. I did not refer to it, though I mentioned it to Alison some weeks later.

This semi-social event was the bright spot of a very gloomy period. Apart from the postal students and the personal compensations of family life with my children — all else proved increasingly disheartening. Church life was quite barren, and Committee members who were supposed to help out with 'chairing', library work, and other duties, were conspicuously absent when the weather was bad or anything tiresome needed to be done. Everything fell on to the shoulders of the few dedicated workers that exist in every church, generally unsung, who keep things going for the rest — and with these I found myself doing more and more small but time-consuming tasks.

Disquietingly, I dreamt that I stood in front of the congregation and talked earnestly to them, trying to gain their attention, but the carpet I stood on writhed beneath my feet like a live thing, and it took much effort to stand upright and keep my balance. The church grew darker, and it seemed to me that the lights were going out everywhere.

Peter had telephoned just after Christmas, and this was the last time he was to contact me. I soon learned the reason. The church caretaker, a kindly middleaged woman, took me aside one Sunday to tell me of things she thought I should know. She was shocked, she said, at the way the healers were speaking behind my back, decrying my advice to Peter and generally making me a laughing stock. I hoped she was exaggerating, but some things she said could only have come via Peter, though I could not believe he would jest about me. I was soon relieved of my illusions. He was back with Mr. K. and "as bad as the rest". "Don't be deceived" she said, looking red and uncomfortable, and repeated the entire conversation.

I have forgotten it now, through the years — but it hurt at the time, for much as I would have preferred to think otherwise, it was all doubtless true and upset me very much. I knew that Peter had tried to break away from old patterns, but ridicule and loss of status had been more than he could face, and his capitulation had been seemingly complete.

In January, too, I developed an abcess in my armpit, something I had never had before, nor since, and for which there was no apparent reason. Painfully it grew for three days and then burst, and I had the ominous feeling that it reflected a pending event.

Shortly before the February Committee meeting, Rose asked me if I would put forward a formal proposition to its members that she should start a group for 'spiritual enfoldment' for the congregation, certain of whom had already suggested it; so I said if she obtained the names of prospective sitters beforehand, I would do so. I felt perturbed about this though I was not sure why, and I wished it hadn't happened.

Rose and I had been friends now for quite a time, and she had proved consistently helpful throughout my term as President. I had never attended any of her groups, but she was of course a professional medium, and both she and her husband had long practised as healers in their own home — she should therefore certainly well know what she was doing. Yet I felt I was responsible for all that was inaugurated during my term of office, and remembered uneasily an occasion when I had visited her socially, and she had suggested that I relax deeply and let myself be used by any spirit present that might wish to communicate. This was standard spiritualist practice, but it caused me to immediately tense in alarm, particularly as I sensed the growing coldness in the room that heralds certain phenomena. I had made some hurried excuse and gone home; nevertheless I tried not to judge or criticise these methods. I hadn't been trained this way, yet conceded there were other ways as well as mine, and it was not for me to query them... and so far our ways had not clashed nor our friendship been put to a test. Knowing the persons Rose had mentioned, all veterans of many circles, I appreciated they were not likely to come to much harm and could certainly benefit from Rose's far wider knowledge than their own.

All would have been well if things had remained this way, but word swiftly went round, and on the Sunday following, a woman approached me to say that she had asked Rose to include her son, a boy of thirteen who was very psychic and whom she felt needed some guidance. I told her he was too young to sit in a group of this nature and that I would not consider letting my own children do this, but she stared at me without comprehension, for Rose, it seemed, had already agreed to take him. Later, Rose gave me a list of proposed sitters, and I saw with consternation that it now included a woman who had recently come out of a mental hospital and was known to suffer hallucinations, also another woman whom I had heard used to 'sit' regularly with friends, and went into spontaneous trances in which she sometimes became violent — once to the extent of trying to strangle a fellow-sitter. Feeling absolutely appalled, I queried them. Rose said she knew them well, and they were perfectly all right. But what about the child? She would take him too.

Hardly believing my ears, I waylaid the friend of the woman reputed to exhibit violence, who confirmed the facts, and added reassuringly that she "wasn't always" like this. But I knew there was no way I could sponsor the involvement of such types in groupwork, though it was too late now to withdraw the matter as it was already on the agenda, and in the secretary's hands for the meeting that evening. Rose knew I had backed out, but she would not retract, thinking me over-anxious about a situation that might never arise.

I faced the stalwart Committee with weak legs and pounding heart, aware that they knew already of Rose's proposition now under scrutiny, and deemed it a good idea — one having said it was high time the Church had a 'circle' again, and inserting her own name on the list along with the rest. I said to them that as President, and thus morally responsible for whatever happened during my term of office, I felt very concerned about certain aspects of the matter under consideration; and carefully stated that three names had been included which I could not affirm, giving my reasons. They looked at me blankly. Rose was a medium, wasn't she? Surely her guides would know what was right or wrong? And surely it was splendid that a child should show interest? We used to have a Lyceum...

I pointed out that there might be influences here that Rose could not control. Swift as a flash she shot out that other people had guides as well as myself, and *her* guides had said it was all right, and that she should include them *all.* I looked at her, and saw the naked emnity in her eyes, and felt the sharp sword of her anger; I was cold and sick inside, shocked at what she revealed — and more so because I knew that she lied.

One by one, and against the rules, I spoke to each of the committee individually, praying that some at least would see sanity. But all solidly backed Rose, whose 'guides' must be wiser than we. They did not understand my concern and put it down to my lack of experience in affairs of mediumship. The vote was taken, myself as sole dissident, and after all other business had been concluded, Rose came over to me, smiling sweetly, and extending her hand to show there was no ill-will. I took it silently, and quickly left.

For several days I wrestled within myself, unwilling to cause further discord, yet knowing inwardly that I could not go on. I had worked at the Presidency as a labour of love and duty, but I could not support what was happening now. With grief I tended my immediate resignation, again giving my reasons. This was accepted without further inquiry, and I learned that Rose was made President in my stead. She sent me a letter saying it was a pity I hadn't come to her groups in the past; I might then have developed as a medium myself.

I notified those concerned that I was relieving Rose of her Brotherhood membership — a decision that Rose described as arbitrary and unfair. Arbitrary it may have been — but it would have been a hypocritical farce to do otherwise. I thought of all the people in the Church of whom I was fond, and who were unlikely to ever hear the truth of this matter, or understand why I had gone; and I cried bitterly at their loss, and the loss of Rose, whom I loved, and of Peter, and Veronica.

My mother, astonishingly, rallied to my support. She had no liking for Rose, and denounced her action strongly to all of her acquaintance. She said other things too, which must have reached Rose's ears but that had no place at all in my reasons for resigning.

Betty, although a Committee member, had not been present at the meeting, and as always when some principle was involved, sat on the fence — comfortably unsure of the rights and wrongs of either party, though she knew quite well the point of issue. She did not wish to lose her position in the Church which a protest against policy would involve, and therefore expediently kept a foot in both camps.

Through Betty I heard that the group soon ran into difficulties and was closed; the reasons were hushed up, and she herself (she said) did not know them despite the fact that Rose was her closest friend. The Secretary also resigned, and Rose took on her job as well. This triple glory apparently cured her of administrative desires, for she did not seek re-nomination. The child incidentally did not go at all; his father wisely intervened and prevented it.

I have included these episodes which in themselves may seem trivial (as one cannot readily communicate the emotions involved) to give prior insight to the recurring situations that continually confronted us. This account has reached the year 1962, and from the vantage point of 1980 a very clear pattern emerges. People were presented again and again with the same issues, whether concealed or readily apparent, and their reactions to certain psychological pressures remained each time as before, my own included. Two persons to my knowledge eventually perceived this, but *could not alter* what they knew to be inadequate responses, for this would necessitate alteration in a whole sequence of attitudes and behaviour patterns which they were either unprepared, or unable then to make.

The somewhat caustic comments sprinkled throughout these pages were not part of the original record made in 1964 — for at that time and during the interim years to 1977 I was unable to use the objective impressions registered and could not confirm them in any acceptable manner. But without doubt we were all given repeated opportunities, the harvest of former lives entirely lost to our memory of today. Yet the opportunity itself, as I saw, could be rendered useless by our lack of preparation in other, less developed, areas of ourselves (which should have been rectified in the time intervening) or through lapses of effort in the current life. One has to keep on the mark, or the fruits of past experience can be nullified, just as the Teachers of old warned repeatedly.

In my sadness at leaving the Church and all its small friendships, I produced a vivid and informative dream. The setting was a large secondary school, and I stood outside the gates watching the pupils gathered in the playground. The gates were locked, and I could not join them much as I wished to. Soon the Master came to fetch me, and led me along a wide column of students waiting admittance to various places of learning. They all wore uniforms denoting their grades, and queued in demarcated sections; at each stage I stopped and stared wistfully at those assembled, and every time I did so the Master shook his head and led me on. Right at the end of the line he silently motioned me to join three girls who waited on the outermost edge. They wore grammar school clothing, brand new, and I realised I was wearing it too. At this point I awoke.

Later that night arose a second dream which appeared to convey the same meaning in a rather different form. It held symbolic subtleties missing in the one earlier, and was as follows: I was alone in a wintry cottage that bordered a still pool. Looking out of its window I perceived that the water was dark and treacherous, and wondered why I had lived there for so long, resolving to leave at once. As I walked past the pool the sun came out, and the trees burst all at once into blossom. It was springtime and the sky was clear and blue.

A lane opened before me, soon narrowing to a sandy path edged by a high wall. This obscured the view and I could not see where I was, or get my bearings. Suddenly I came to a pit, not very deep, and about the size of a man, though it wasn't a grave. It filled the width of the path and I greatly feared I should fall into it as I tried to pass, but unseen hands held my feet, and guided them carefully along the perilous strip between wall and pit that permitted one step only at a time, and I thus kept my balance. Having passed the pit safely, the wall abruptly ceased, and I was then in the centre of a town at the junction of a cross-roads. Along the main highway, from East to West, marched a long procession of people. They were of many races and all were singing, and as they drew closer I recognised them — they were *my* people, to whom I belonged — and I joined them, singing with all my heart. And here I awoke, knowing the dream to be precognitive.

There were no group meetings at all throughout January or February, as every time I tried to arrange one it consistently fell through. The impression of gathering darkness experienced before leaving the Church was still with me, but its implication was essentially different. The former was tinged with the apprehension of trouble ahead from the outside — but this latter darkness was my own — the reflection of an inner loneliness and despair akin to a sense of abandonment. This steadily increased, and linked in my awareness with the strange inner yearning of eighteen months ago; yet it did not intrude into my daily life, which continued as before.

Joan's baby, a little girl, was born early in February after an alarming time for all concerned, for everything possible went wrong in the latter stages of her pregnancy, and it was feared at one point that neither Joan or the then unborn child would survive. Mercifully they did, and after some days she wrote to me from hospital with all her former affection and said that when she was stronger she hoped to rejoin us again. Her letter was like a shaft of light and I read it many times over.

Late in February Alison, worn out with vigil, sent word that she too, would soon be with us, and asked for typing that could be done at home as her contribution to the postal work. This was immensely helpful for I was snowed under with three different courses to complete, and numerous enquiries. In March we were joined by another postal student who also worked well and conscientiously, but with him I had no feeling of connection. He seemed to have slipped in from the outer, more orthodox world, and did not draw close like the rest.

Margaret arrived one evening looking utterly exhausted from overlong nursing of a bed-ridden friend, and I visited Lois who had coped all winter with a sick sister and was thinner and very overtired. Ann managed an evening away from elderly and ailing aunts, and Betty likewise. They were all warmly interested in the postal students, so I linked them by letter — Margaret with Mary, Joan with Phillip, Lois with Vera...

Patrick had reacted strongly to the increased pressure of work, although it didn't involve contact, and there were no meetings and I had no more evenings at the Church. He hated to find me typing when he came home, and having no inside work at the moment for the dark early evenings, took far more note of my activities.

I realised I had begun to detach myself from Patrick despite our being quite happy together of late. We always got on well when I gave him my full attention and kept my life exclusively domestic, and it was frustrating that even the smallest departure from this created problems. I had tried so often to interest him even superficially in my personal life to no avail, and it was now that I finally accepted that his attitudes would never change, and frequently felt torn inside by my deep wish to please him and my inner, conflicting need to grow.

Several times I felt a strange sensation enter my head, as if impressions were being crammed into it which somehow or other would have to release themselves into my life. A distressing, even frightening factor was that they were unlike any impressions registered before; my life was too limited and constricted to contain them and I did not know what to do with their stirring. It seemed a new life cried out to me, with new events and new experiences; and the pressures engendered were like trying to force a quart into a pint jug.

Days went by and still nothing moved. The brief emergence of individuals was but an interlude, for of necessity each returned to their burdened lives and again were absorbed by the same vicissitudes. All I had instigated in faith and hope appeared ill-judged and untimely. The many letters of enquiry bore no fruit, and four students only were the end result of my regular advertisements. This I knew was not as it should be, for the literature was sound and the fees very substantially lower than anything remotely equivalent. Even my dream life slowed down to almost nil, reflecting the general impasse of events.

The only light in this dark period came from the postal students; and one in particular, the schoolteacher, responded so strongly that it soon became obvious he was focussing his attention on the School and the impetus he felt behind it. His thoughts were concentrated, and I felt their flow as a warm stream, wondering at first if I imagined this, then convinced beyond doubt that I did not.

Among his letters were sprinklings of personal detail; he had married late in life a few years previously a girl much younger than himself, and they now had a baby daughter. His concepts were oddly Victorian, and even more unrealistically idealistic than my own had been. I sensed his marriage had not yielded the affinity he sought, and how deeply this had affected him — appreciating suddenly that the toughening process I had undergone had been much to my advantage, for it made me far less vulnerable to shattered illusions.

One morning on waking I saw clairvoyantly a rain of letters pushed through the letterbox, a dozen at least, and knew that they were all from Philip — but these were personal letters, nothing to do with his course, and a tremor of shock passed through me. Even so, this was not as it might seem, for he wrote to me as if he assumed I was a mature and middleaged lady of some erudition — whereas I was still but thirtythree, non-academic, and not all that mature as I can now see.

The peculiar blackness that clung to me intensified systematically, and I grasped that I was entering, not the darkness of depressing events, but a kind of black light — or light so pure that I was unable to register it. It was tenuous, rarified, fine... and at its heart was a longing, agonisingly deep, that I merely touched upon. This light had a penetrative effect and activated layers of inner life that I had not known existed; but it was all *unseen*, and so obscure — a dark ante-room to birth into a stratum entirely and utterly different to the terrestial. This confused me, and worst of all, the waning interior guidance of the past few months now ceased completely. The light eclipsed, and I was lost and desolate.

In the first days of April I reached a nadir so impenetrable and acute it caused many solitary tears. Each day had become an ordeal that must be endured rather than lived through; and at night I lay wakeful, knowing my aloneness, and that my Companion was no longer there. I had not realised the completeness of my dependence upon Him, for when He withdrew I was a rudderless ship.

Sitting alone one evening, with Patrick out and the children in bed, I gradually became aware of a light growing within and around me, which lifted my consciousness to such an extent that I realised I was again in the Master's Presence; and within this awareness was the knowledge that I had not been forsaken, nor mistaken in my efforts. I understood that the process of attunement was still incomplete, and I must strive now to attain a finer degree of comprehension, and a level of communication only briefly sustained previously. For many hours that night I lay awake, the light flowing continuously into my mind; ideas, impressions and decisions filtering into my brain and struggling there for form and manifestation. I registered anew the Master's emanation, not as formerly, for here was no tangibility, and the vibration so swift, so delicate, so ultra-refined, I did not know with the same clarity as before if I had grasped what was required. A combined effort pitched to a higher frequency appeared necessary. Tentatively I formulated a design. Unity was as always the objective, and all else merely means to that end.

The following day I set in motion a little of what had come to me, and contacted each of the remaining Brotherhood, outlining a linking five-minute meditation to take place nightly, wherever one might be, at 9.15. In this we would visualise the garden of our former exercise and follow its paths to the central sanctuary, there to heighten our aspiration, and project the colour individually given, into the translucent canopy above — creating thus on more subtle levels a structure that I saw would in some form externalise. They all responded, glad I think, to do something constructive at last about our seemingly non-existent group relationship. And curiously... it worked. Of their own accord they gave more time than specified, and each evening the seven colours of the spectrum were transmitted with varying strengths, and the efficacy of this was soon apparent.

It was Betty's task as the most mediumistic among us to observe its actualisation, and herself project and reinforce whatever was most lacking. Before long she reported there were definite stains of colour overhead — then that yellow was consistently weak or missing altogether, and Joan (who had been given yellow) admitted that sometimes she was just too tired at the end of the day to either meditate or to visualise effectively.

Rupert, who was using red, soon dropped out through other commitments, and Betty took it instead. But she wasn't happy with its stimulus, nor with the violet we interchanged; so nightly I alternated their projection and Betty continued with her former task.

From mid-April the group again met weekly, and re-established former work patterns as if the blockages that bound us had been released. Everyone exerted themselves with renewed spirit, and once more we drew together as closely as ever, and the meetings continued productively until mid-July. Our activities included our second Brotherhood function, for most of us attended the christening of baby Rachel and returned to Joan's home afterwards. It was a delightful experience — warm, friendly and aspirational. Joan's husband, Ian, made us all very welcome, and we felt for those hours like a closely-knit family.

Since the night when vision was restored to me, I had experienced a brilliant light in the central region of my head. This was in effect, the result of over-stimulation, and at times it grew quite overpowering. It lasted about a fortnight and then gradually subsided, leaving the feeling that I had been 'tuned-up' in some way, like a stringed instrument, and now needed time to adjust to this hyper-sensitive level. But as always, there *was* no time, and one had to manage as best one could. Necessity perhaps ultimately proved the best balance, for I was compelled to polarise by the needs of my family and the sheer pressure of obligations.

My dream life recommenced, and provided a cameo in which I waited with others at a bus-stop on a quiet country road; a vehicle drew up and we all boarded it. I knew we were going somewhere of great importance to everyone concerned. A few days later I awoke to see, clairvoyantly, the same bus-stop; but I stood there alone. An empty, single-decker coach drew alongside, and I entered it and was its sole passenger. Both perceptions, though similar, appeared to denote different events, for they carried differing vibrations — yet were connected by a common factor, the starting point or bus-stop.

During April I contacted our still strongly aspiring student and gave him a more accurate outline of the situation than he obviously held in his mind. I felt it wrong to let him continue with his imaginative view of us, and I also told him my age and of my somewhat limited background experience — though he knew from the lectures that my inner experience, at least, was considerable. I asked if he would like to join with us in our colour meditation, leaving aside the one he was doing — and if so to project red for us in place of Rupert, who showed no sign of taking it up again. But there was no reply at the expected time — no worksheets either; nor did he write to Joan.

From December onwards his letters had been frequent and regular, and he had worked and studied more rapidly than the others. I feared now I had so shocked him by my disclosure that, disheartened, he had left. Yet the thought-stream continued as before — at times agitated, and there seemed a definite attempt to turn away and disconnect himself. Without his response there was nothing further I could do, so I turned my attention elsewhere for there was always plenty to engage it.

On May 13th, in sleep I experienced an extension of consciousness into another dimension. I was again the Self of the white robe, existent in a non-physical state that remained linked to, and aware of, my sleeping body. Spread before me in space, yet also *within* me, and encompassed in a circle of Time — my evolution unfurled. I saw my initial separation from the Formless Oneness that was the Master Unmanifest, and the cyclic growth that followed — and witnessed this same process happening to other souls and the essential oneness of humanity. Locked in the curving Cycle I observed the terrible suffering that had been allotted me, and cried out in terror — but strong arms bore me up, and I was shown that the time of tribulation had passed — I had already gone through the 'fire'... today I should be 'crowned', for the circle neared its completion. I saw then a male form clad also in white moving swiftly towards me. We each ascended opposite sides of an arc — and at the summit I knew we should meet in such union that separation could be no more — I should be one with him forever.

This experience affected me profoundly. I had perceived and comprehended a great Mystery, the secret that lies enshrined at the heart of all Universal Life. I registered it clearly, powerfully, impactively; then its meaning was withdrawn and veiled or covered over, and all efforts to retrieve it proved in vain. In its stead, the light that infused me in early April inflowed again, and was so bright and intense my head and nervous system were charged to their limit, and I moved through the days in a condition of deep absorption. As I assimilated this, it astounded me that Patrick was unaware of my changed condition — yet he was, though he grew increasingly annoyed by my preoccupation with affairs and problems other than his own.

I began to taste the coming difficulties of my marital situation. It had taken all my time and efforts, and the inner discipline of years to achieve family harmony in the first place; now the inner pull was proving slightly disruptive — there were cracks in the smooth surface of our life together and I could not see where it would end. I looked at Patrick, feeling sad and rather afraid, and understood in some part of me that our fourteenth anniversary, in March, had marked the end of a phase.

It was a month before Phillip replied to my letter, saying yes, he would be pleased to join us. He commented rather lamely that he had been inundated with work, and now had more time again. And certainly he projected red, for Betty pronounced that suddenly the canopy was flooded with it, submerging our more delicate hues — a factor I had perceived myself. I wrote requesting a modulation, which was promptly complied with, indicating a very real ability to control mentation. He write back at once this time, a letter unlike those sent formerly, being longer and much more personal; following this swiftly with a second and third.

I noted now a disturbing quality at the time of the meditation period, for he seemed to be there beside me, almost tangibly so. His thoughts were upon me, and with incredulity I registered his tenderness — it was as though his arms were about me, and he cried... oh, how he cried. Deeply troubled, I persuaded myself I was imagining this — distorting perhaps a potent expression of aspirational friendship; but it grew stronger, emotive beyond the bounds of imagination, until his thoughts were quite unmistakable. Betty observed cautiously that he seemed no longer with us as before, though he still projected his red — she felt he had somehow refocussed himself... perhaps upon me?

This I knew was correct, and it frightened me, for I could not escape him; yet what he exuded was also a balm, seeping into my pent-up soul — reaching out to an untouched depth within me, stirring it from sleep. And here I could have made a most serious error with the greatest of ease. Unknown to myself there were two assignations immediately ahead of me, of quite different nature, for quite different purposes; though the lesser linked with the greater, and was under its aegis.

So potent were these impressions one evening that I found myself spontaneously translating them — reproducing their impulses in semi-visual form... a sedate Victorian setting; a piano, a young woman wearing a dress of green silk... And above the delicate notes, a man's light voice singing "On wings of song I'll bear thee..." with such poignancy it touched my heart.

I could not believe my senses, and yet it was so; and the next evening it happened again. At length, pierced to the depths, I wrote to him with much apprehension, wording my letter with the utmost care and asking discreetly if he had tried to communicate with me telepathically, and why this nostalgic scene? Did I indeed imagine the green dress and the plaintive song? I cannot recall how I expressed it — I placed my trust in the gentle prompting that had never betrayed me, for this was foreign soil and only the Master could guide me safely through the vortex I saw ahead.

A letter arrived by return, expressed with equal delicacy and an underlying ardour. No, it had not been imagined — it was all as I had seen; the piano, the girl, the dress, the song — and also the tears. And more than this, for I had not said all. And the 'more' contained the things I had sensed, and things that I knew from my own imperfect glimpses of a long distant past, way beyond the last century.

I had known him before beyond doubt — here were memories shared, or so I assumed. I must have loved him, and lost him — by death? His, or mine? Maybe through war? I could not recall, but emotion welled up within me, and I sat on the stairs still holding his letter and cried grievously. It was so futile, so impossible — to connect with a love long dead, to a person unknown and unseen, in the midst of fresh lives and committed relationships.

We exchanged more letters and I learned the reason for his month of silence. He had 'known', he said, when he got my letter — and had tried to turn away, to retrieve himself from the emotional havoc he knew was otherwise inevitable. But he could not do it, his need was too strong. He described his early memories of a woman much loved, whom he had looked for fruitlessly in his youth, and thought at last he had found in his young wife, though, too late, he realised his mistake. He wrote of his work-filled years in the cloistered world of boarding school — his narrow bachelordom, and insipid marriage — and the terrible shock to his consciousness when his dream erupted into an inferno of feeling in the spring... as if the open door of memory had let through a residual grief and passion from the unfinished past that had overwhelmed him. Through his words I felt his love stream out in an anguished surge to reach me, pouring over me like a flood, saturating my aura till I hardly knew my own feelings from his. Indeed, I don't think I knew them at all; I merely reflected back his own projections.

My mind was like a receiving station — attuned to his every claim upon it. My knowledge of music was small, yet he transmitted to me the loveliest piano solos and entire symphonies and orchestrations. One night I could not sleep at all, so quickened was my receptivity by the rapport he established. He confirmed by letter his own wakefulness, and verified repeatedly the accuracy of my registrations.

This was the point where, if left to my own devices, I could have confused the incoming impressions, having seen that experiences in our lives are filtered through to us as impulses before emerging into manifestation. These impulses can be perceived in a certain state of awareness and registered as precognitions — and I had already foreseen my own awakening to an all-consuming love.

To make things more complex, in June came another vivid sleep experience; I was in a dark place, in some state that was located in my head, yet at the same time existent on a mental level far above the grossity of the earth. I saw my Self — She of the white robe — positioned above me with only her own light to illuminate the gloom, and was simultaneously aware of my supine physical body, and my consciousness (which was observing) in some intermediate stratum.

There was a thread connecting the glowing Self with the lesser form, and my consciousness, like a nucleus, appeared to be moving along the thread into the finer body. She was still, as if bound, but straining agonisingly to reach someone, and I saw another figure, also incredibly beautiful — exuding light, and wearing a white garment — moving with great effort towards her. I remember his face clearly — he was young, as was she, and he loved her as she did him, with such divine power and intensity that I could hardly bear it. His hands reached out to touch her — he scarcely moved, but the effort involved was terrible to see. Suddenly his light met hers, and there was a mighty sound that was wordless and silent, yet charged with such dynamic potency I felt a severe electric shock, and my consciousness was precipitated back along the thread into my body with shattering propulsion. In the split second it took — the silent sound became words as it penetrated the mental strata; she had cried "Mazda!", and he had cried "Veritas!" I learned later they meant Light and Truth. The brilliance of their auras affected me for several days.

In the back of my mind I knew that this could not be connected with Phillip, and it was soon confirmed in the purposeful, unsentimental and wholely compassionate way I long knew I must heed. I had glimpsed an affinitive Eden and cried helplessly with longing for that union of mind denied me, asking at last of the Master if I might have the love that seemed offered, though it must be platonic — and after a while I sensed the presence of the nun, Teresa, whose loving warmth embraced me as surely as if she had drawn close in the flesh to comfort me — but her counsel was of the hardest kind for me to accept. Her voice breathed into my mind on its silent vibration. "It cannot be. Try not to grieve". I was choked with tears, for I knew I could not have what I thought I most wanted.

I longed to tell someone of this bewildering influx — to share it with a sympathetic viewpoint, but a few brief words spoken to Joan on the subject convinced me this was folly. Any mention of such unsought subtleties was construed at once as marital disloyalty, so I kept it to myself. When in 1964/65 I included the following facts in my original m.s., I reaped nothing but censure — and aspersions that followed me through the years, adding fuel to other fires. I therefore submit them for what they are to the more discerning eyes for whom these pages were written.

For some while I had thought of visiting one or more of the small Centres in London to see how they functioned, and decided first on the White Eagle Lodge of which I had heard good reports. There was a little money now of my own for such purposes, Patrick having made very good profits. He had made me a loan to float the schoolwork and had recently said I need not repay it, so I arranged the visit for early June, but was unwell on the chosen weekend and had to cancel it. I mentioned this to Phillip in a letter and said I would try again soon. I had no thought at all of seeing him there, as his school was in Surrey and he was, of course, much married.

On Saturday of the week following, I answered the telephone to hear a strange male voice asking to speak to me, knowing at once who it was. It so happened, he said, that he had a special examination course to attend in London the coming week, and if I could synchronise times perhaps we could meet at the Lodge? He emphasised it might well prove our only opportunity to talk privately with each other, for on his intended visit to Cambridge in August we would meet as a group.

I trembled from head to foot. It was one thing on paper, or in thought, to be in contact with another man — but in reality? To my amazement Patrick that same afternoon decided on impulse to take a few days holiday and go home, and was soon packed and ready to leave in his usual whirlwind fashion. My uncertainty suddenly dissolved and I made up my mind to go on the Wednesday whilst he was away, arranging with my sister-in-law to have the children after school. She knew that I never went anywhere, and laughingly said it would do me good to have a break and there was no need to hurry back — the children could sleep overnight with her — she'd love to have them. So for the first time in years the usual pressures were removed from me, and deeply convinced me that it was necessary to meet Phillip however alarming I might feel about it.

There was a further phone call Tuesday evening to enquire the time of my train — he would like to meet me by car. Patrick also telephoned to say he would be staying the full week. He knew of my visit to London and I told him that I hoped to meet Mr. G. at the Lodge, also that he was now thinking of coming to Cambridge to make contact with the others on Friday. Patrick swore and said in that case he'd take care to be away until Saturday; he had no wish to be involved in any social function. As Tuesday was our groupnight I made the arrangement there and then for everyone to be present on Friday afternoon.

That night I dreamt of what would occur, and its aftermath; the information passing vaguely through my mind without impact, as if it had been 'screened' to prevent a reaction, or as if some part of me did not really wish to know. It also clearly revealed that Phillip, in truth, was a student — who would vacate my life as suddenly as he had entered it. But I could not bear to believe it just then, and pushed the thought aside.

I travelled to Liverpool Street station in a daze, wondering how I would feel when I met him, and how he would look... and if our recognition would be immediate and mutual. A man stood at the barrier, slim and dark — transparently nervous, very intense. My heart sank... he was not as I had imagined him. Here was no shoulder to lean on, no tower of strength in which to confide — but another Patrick, another Peter... greatly in need himself and quite unable to sustain someone else in his turn. I hid my disappointment for I saw it was not mutual. He took my hand and was obviously deeply moved.

Once in his car a raw panic rose in me. I did not know him. He was a stranger, an unknown quantity, and I could not recognise the student, much less the man who had projected so much love. His face was pale and harrassed, looking older than his years, and if we had met in the normal course of life he would not have attracted me in the slightest. He glanced at me repeatedly as if assessing my reactions, and made halting conversation as we probed the London traffic. He wished to talk, and I knew we must get it over with before going on to the Lodge. As we moved towards the city outskirts I thought longingly of Patrick, for he was all I knew of men and represented safety. But I need not have been so fearful. With swift inner certainty I knew suddenly that no harm would befall me, and the panic subsided. Secure in this knowledge I took a deep breath and my system began slowly to relax.

We found a grass verge and sat by the roadside well back from the noisy intrusion of endless transport. Birds were singing in the trees behind us, and the sun shone warmly. It was a lovely day, but the tension between us was such that we could neither of us fully enjoy it. He, like myself, was too shaped by duty and convention to really unwind, a fact which in retrospect made the whole situation almost incredible. Despite his shyness he told me by degrees the story of his life, with all its hopes and fears and privations. Being in the right age group he had caught the full brunt of the war, and had served with the army in France. Constant confrontation with death and his own miraculous survival, though wounded, had long convinced him that his life was meaningful, and he had sought inwardly his own source deeply and sincerely in the manner of all aspirants.

From time to time he looked hesitantly at me, his eyes entreating me not to reject him, and as I listened I found I could gradually see the inner man emerge — the man who had written me so many letters. It was strangely moving yet quite impersonal, for I felt nothing emotionally. My feelings were frozen by inhibited fear and past conditioning. I can see now that I was just as locked up as he.

At length we went to the Lodge and talked with other visitors, then sat for a long while in the chapel, holding hands and silent — both aware of the tranquil stillness and an undertone of sorrow, as if we had passed through some great sadness together like the loss of a child.

It was late when we left, and Phillip suggested I stay overnight near London and we could meet again the following day — he could get round the course work. I had not intended this and had no overnight things with me, not even a toothbrush; but I knew that whatever I had come for had not so far occurred, so I agreed, phoning my sister-in-law who at once put my mind at ease.

He took me to his mother's home, quite certain she would accommodate me; but welcoming though she was I could see it wasn't as convenient as he had thought, and by now it was almost time he was home himself. Hastily he booked me in at a small hotel by the roadside, very old and picturesque, and left swiftly, saying he would be back again in the morning.

How I enjoyed that night! My mind was too active to sleep, and I sat up in bed eating chocolate and reading the literature brought from the Lodge, luxuriating in the unaccustomed sense of freedom. In the early hours of the morning I drifted serenely into sleep, blissfully relaxed at last and completely at peace in the cosy old room; but a dream soon dispelled the deep happiness that had stolen upon me — for in it Patrick came to fetch me, angry and disturbed, chiding me mercilessly for my friendship with another man; and I cried bitterly, heartbrokenly, for some reason lost as I awoke.

Phillip arrived on time, and we repeated the events of the previous day feeling much more at ease with each other, and slowly I found myself thawing towards him as his natural self became more apparent. It was hard for me to believe he was married. His manner was rather rigid — he had the air of a man unfamiliar with women, and this evoked in me a subtle worldliness that helped draw him out of his shell. As time passed we talked freely together, and found so much to say over such a wide range that I quite forgot he was a stranger, projecting a vibrant aspect of myself that had never surfaced before.

The day passed quickly, and late afternoon found us wedged in traffic as we fruitlessly sought the premises of the Arcane School. I had expressed the wish to visit their library and to see for myself something of the organisation that had so influenced and affected me in the past. At last we gave up, and instead went once more to the Lodge, and again, with regret, I prepared to go home. Phillip looked at me hopelessly — we had talked so much but still there was so much to say, and heaven knew when we would get a further opportunity. Watching each other we both knew the episode was unfinished, that there was something more to come — we had not yet reached the point and purpose of our meeting. I decided again to stay on; we would find some quiet place to talk over what could not be said before. He phoned his wife and made an excuse about delay; I phoned my sister-in-law. She informed me, to my distress, that Patrick was back unexpectedly. He had left her a message to give me if I should think of remaining away longer — it being that he wished me to return *immediately*. The house felt so empty, he'd told her, and he was rather upset that I wasn't there, but the children were still with her, and perfectly happy.

My world overturned. Immediately fearful, my first impulse was to catch the next train... yet I did not feel able to face him so soon, merged as I was with the aura of Phillip, and acutely aware now of my own conflicting emotions. He left me as and when he chose, not bothering himself with how I felt, or if I was lonely or distressed. This wasn't the point of course, as I well knew — and certainly I had no wish to make him miserable. But I was convinced that something remained unresolved and felt I could not leave until it was. I said I would be home first thing in the morning, that there was someone here I wished to talk with first. As Patrick was out I left the message with my sister-in-law.

We found a quiet guesthouse and Phillip came to my room, where at last there was privacy and we were alone together. He had migraine, he said unhappily, doubtless caused by stress, for after Patrick's request he felt as wretched as myself. To do as we were doing in such a clandestine manner was alien to us both; yet the guiding impetus that had brought us to this juncture knew better than we the purposes it served. The ice had been broken, a relationship formed... and now we could speak of more intimate things — the thoughts he had sent me, the Victorian room, the music... the memories from the past... And suddenly it was as if we had entered another age — as if time slipped back, and we were two different people who had loved one another and been torn apart.

Something within him, deeply repressed, moved beneath the surface of consciousness, and rose spontaneously outside his volition in an upwelling of anguished and tender emotion — a reprojection of the intensity of loss and grief, the pain of curbed and unfulfilled love. In stumbling words, forgotten now, he spoke to that other woman, unlocking the choked-up fount in his mind and feelings, releasing trapped images long imprisoned. It was like a catharsis, and when it subsided he inwardly withdrew from me, though I don't think he realised this — and I knew then that the dream he had lived in for so long had come to an end, and he had turned himself homewards. I felt exhausted and sad; reluctant to part from him, yet aware he had gone from me already. His manner was gentle and loving but much less personal; he said he could not bear to come to Cambridge tomorrow after all, he felt too shattered, and to meet again so soon... We parted at last, and I felt more for him when we said goodbye than at any time since we met.

It is so easy here to give the wrong impression. It was a subtle release he sought — a need to pierce the walled-up emotion of a lifetime, to dissolve the images that acted as a barrier to his life of today. He knew this himself, and whatever his personal feelings as a man, there had been no suggestion of anything more. Steeped as we both were in idealistic concepts, with the minds of our partners upon us, the awareness of dearly loved children — there had been no question of adultery; just the need for understanding, and to reach out to another, essence to essence, in that strange, twilit land of the suffering soul — a fact that others have found hard to believe, or have blatantly disbelieved, as I found to my cost.

I returned feeling dreadful, my thoughts unable to move away from Phillip, whom I knew was thinking of me, and my whole being reflecting the impact of what had transpired. I had scarcely slept at all and felt utterly worn out. The pain in my back which always came with psychic drainage made me feel ill, and I longed only to get to bed and to be alone.

Patrick was distraught; he had not slept either — the house was "empty and dead" without myself and the children. He was vulnerable and demanding, overwhelmingly possessive, and he asked a hundred questions about every detail of my stay. In my heart I cried without cease, for it was all too much for me — first Phillip's emotions, then Patrick's, and now my own. I felt I had been shipwrecked in a storm; and worse still, my conviction of purpose had gone, and it seemed that nothing constructive had happened at all.

The others had to be contacted and the afternoon's meeting cancelled. I talked brightly and gave no indication of the anguish I felt, and at last things wound down and life returned to normal. Well almost; for two things happened which were in no sense part of the daily round, and both piled on the emotional conflict and inner pain that proved the first faint foreshadowings of the next two years of test and trial.

In the week following my return from London, Patrick delivered me an ultimatum. I must give up the school and the postal work, and also the groups. He didn't want this kind of thing in his life, nor visitors to his home, and certainly not men, who in his estimation were all cranks to bother with such things. It had all gone too far and got out of hand. And he didn't want a woman who was psychic and had all these dreams — he wanted a *real* woman, one who wanted the things *he* wanted; and if I didn't do as he wished — it meant the end of our marriage, for he would leave me.

I felt stunned about this, having had no inkling of what was in his mind, and frightened too, for I knew he was serious, and that I could not, of my own accord, comply. I tried to explain to him, to express how much it all meant to me, but he would hear none of it. I had known what he was like when I married him he protested — it was *I* that had changed, not he. And *I* must put this right.

For three days he bullied and harrassed me, coming home at odd times when the children were at school and reducing me to a state of guilt and wretchedness. I cried and implored but he was quite adamant. An ultimatum it was, and he would not withdraw it.

In the end I said that much as I loved him, I could not do what he wanted — for even if I tried, there would be something else — I could not live like a cabbage, and it would happen all over again. It wasn't possible to change myself; I had always been the same, but he had been too otherwise involved to find this out — he only knew now through reading the lectures he'd helped to duplicate, or maybe he had paused long enough in his worklife to reassess me — I didn't know.

More likely, of course, he had subconsciously registered my concern with another man. Whatever the reason, he in his turn was shattered by my reaction. Having pushed me to extremity, he couldn't credit that for once he had not come first. Throughout our marriage his needs and wants had been my foremost consideration, and it was more than he could apprehend that I should now refuse so utterly to please him. He felt suddenly unsure of himself, and to my even greater distress, betrayed his own vulnerability and dependence. As always, I tried to comfort him; and for a while we went on as before.

The second thing, concurrent but quite separate, was the unexpected aftermath of my contact with Phillip, of which I told no-one at all. For immediately following my return I had begun to experience an appalling state of desire — an intensity of passion that held me in its grip for almost a fortnight and filled me literally with terror. It was more than a stupendous backfiring of emotion; and different in essence to the crystallisation of an excess of stimulative light. Never had I experienced anything of its nature previously — it was of a strength and potency quite foreign to myself, and caused me agonies of shame and distress. I knew intuitively that it was subtle in origin and could not be expressed in any physical form; nor anyway would I have attempted this. It had no link with my marriage, or Patrick, nor for that matter with Phillip, for our relationship had been either mental or emotional. I could only eventually conclude I had absorbed it from him on a subtle level, in a highly concentrated form, and must in some way 'burn-up' or transmute it. But such comforting reflections were fleeting, and I felt full of misery and guilt for this hitherto unknown facet of myself, which all my years of aspirational striving had not overcome.

I learned much later that a Master will often relieve his pupils of such unwanted impressions that might sidetrack them or cause obstacles to their inner development. That in many aspirants there are blocs of impulses of varying types still existent in the subtle body — perhaps left over from the forgotten past, and waiting but the opportunity to again express themselves. By taking these upon himself and transmuting them, he thus prevents the karmic backswing that perpetuates their life, nullifying them completely. And sometimes he may use another pupil to facilitate this as part of their training for future work — or merely as an intermediary for his own. In this particular instance it is likely that both things happened, as was indicated in due time.

Phillip wrote twice after our meeting, assuring me of his continued depth of feeling and insisting that nothing had changed; but his words had a hollow ring and I did not believe them. I continued with the meditation and soon realised I was alone — that neither Phillip, nor anyone else, was there. Upon enquiry the group, strangely enough, admitted that each one had neglected it under the erroneous impression that the others continued as before, and it therefore would not matter. I made no attempt to rally them; it seemed the impetus had gone. They were all working harmoniously and well in other ways, and I left it at that. But I tuned in myself until quite sure that Phillip's intermittent efforts had ceased altogether. In the meantime there were no more letters, and no worksheets.

After five weeks of silence he wrote again and returned all his books, explaining his reasons. To express it briefly, he and his wife had drawn suddenly closer through a series of rather unusual incidents, and their relationship now showed more promise than at any time since their marriage. He hoped I would understand. She was, however, averse to his studies, and for the time being he felt he should leave them aside; he sent his love and said he would write again soon.

He didn't, of course. The dream was finally over. I grieved silently and deeply for the frailty of love, and gradually the heartache faded, leaving me at the summer's end sadder and wiser, but myself again.

Among the many vivid dreams recorded now, was one in which I wore a blue Edwardian nightgown and lay in a hospital bed awaiting a tonsil operation. Outside was an earthen compound reminding me of India, and soon I stood in its centre with the dark, vital man I had seen before, who talked to me with great animation. He had brought me a communication from the Master, which for some reason caused me to thrust my hand through a glass barrier, successfully breaking it, but leaving my right palm covered with blood that I stared at uncomprehendingly.

Having long ago lost my tonsils I concluded the earlier part of the dream referred to the throat chakra, with which I have always associated the colour blue and the registration of sound and vibration. I felt too, that this centre had a specific linkage with the one at the base of the spine relating to human sexuality. But I could not link these clues together in a meaningful way, and the whole dream disturbed me, for I knew it was precognitive.

Another dream, extremely vivid, found me sweeping away autumn leaves in a tree-lined street named Pilgrims Way. The colouring throughout was breathtaking, the very epitome of autumnal grandeur. I had cleared the debris of summer, and logs and twigs were neatly stacked and tied back along the roadside.

Everything had been done and all was tidied and in order. I was then in my own kitchen sweeping five pretty ladybirds into a new dustpan. These I gently placed outside the rear door, from which point they all made off in different directions.

During the third week in July I was insistently impressed to discontinue the group meetings. This was most puzzling as they were fully attended and very productive, and I wondered if the current pressures of my personal life were creating a distortion. I decided, uncertainly, to let another week pass before mentioning it, but on that particular Tuesday the matter was taken out of my hands. Before the meeting commenced, Joan told us Ian's job was moving them suddenly to a village outside the city, within the fortnight in fact, and she would thus lose her kindly baby-sitter and find it impossible to join us unless Ian was off-duty. Margaret then said she had just accepted the care of another invalid and had felt that for the time being she would have to leave us... Lois looked up and murmured something similar, adding that her decision had reluctantly been taken before she arrived; and Betty announced that she and Rupert were arranging a private group for Church members as he was now President, and she had been worrying how she could manage both... Ann, we knew already, was moving temporarily from the city in September to take a course in Leeds.

It was plain we were once again saying goodbye, and I told them then of my promptings to conclude the present meetings, also of the persistent impressions that there was something new arising that I didn't yet know of... which it would be necessary to connect with, as near as I could date it in the third week of September — a 'something' that I felt might not interest them in the same way it would absorb myself. And of the curious glimpse several times of myself and Alison 'running parallel' as if on a circular track... Alison laughed, for she had recently been made President of the T.S. — the former President having emigrated; and the likelihood of myself joining the T.S. was remote. We all sat quietly thinking of what the future held for us, and then the serious moment passed and we settled to enjoy our last time together as a group.

Before we separated, Alison told us laughingly of a peculiar incident which had happened that day. A few nights previously she had dreamt a man entered her bedroom and raised her by the hand and kissed her, asking if she remembered where and when they had met before — and "Lo and behold", at lunchtime a voluble young Indian gentleman had arrived on her doorstep enquiring about the Theosophical Lodge, and she'd had the strange impression he was "one and the same man". I stared at her — some intuition stirred within me, profoundly affective, but it swiftly subsided.

Patrick was delighted by the group's closure, and thought his ultimatum had at last sunk in and caused me to act accordingly. He did an unheard of thing and voluntarily suggested we buy more furniture, which certainly we could do with; but it was saddening to me that he thought this would take the place of my inner life, and pleased though I was, it did not alter the fact that all the riches in the world could not bridge the gulf I saw between us.

His mother, a dear old lady, came to visit us for a week, and was immensely interested and involved with the house, the garden, the furniture, T/V... and Patrick watched me unceasingly, aware at last that however I behaved outwardly, these things were not as meaningful to *me* — they did not come *first.* And every now and then he attacked me angrily for my lack of normality, in private of course — and reduced me to tears.

September came and the days stretched emptily ahead. I missed the group and wondered why it had been taken away from me. The postal work was all up to date, and my former certitude of new things entering my life had completely disappeared. I queried rather desperately how I would manage to live in this vacuum that Patrick desired of me, and knew despairingly that I could not. I would die, or have a breakdown. Only my children brought colour and joy into life; for with Patrick, love him as I undoubtedly did — the knowledge that everything stopped for his pub, and that his habits were totally inflexible, was more than defeating.

My dreams were disturbing — graphic as ever they related some future event to my brain not readily grasped. Time and again I found myself with someone dearly loved, who led me through a maze of improbable situations which were quite beyond my ability to translate into possible occurrences. Of the many lesser, and separate, indications — I will pinpoint a few, to give a little idea of the current complexity.

(a) My mother, in Egyptian(?) robes, tried to poison me with asps — then placed a serpent in my path.

(b) I was shown a deep canal of dark green water with a grille rising from it, and told (not in relation to myself) that when this place was reached people usually committed suicide, but "it would not be so this time".
(c) I stood, griefstricken, in a dim setting, crying as if my heart would break, and a dark-eyed man pointed consolingly to my inheritance, which shone brightly some distance ahead through the darkness.
(d) I tried to listen to an urgent voice instructing me amid a rising babble all around. I strained to catch the words, and attempted to persuade others to still themselves and listen with me, but they all had mundane tasks they wished to perform, and the noise and confusion grew rapidly worse.
(e) I walked in a dark place, crying and crying, yet did not know why. A young man watched me from the shadows and tried to reassure me. I asked him, "Please, can you tell me why I am crying?" but his reply was lost as I awoke.
(f) I found myself telling the group that I was to be married, then looked at the wedding photos and saw myself as a weeping bride, crying so much there were pools of tears all over the ground. The scene was the earthen compound observed in previous dreams; the bridegroom was hidden, and the bride was heavily pregnant. I did not know how to explain this at all to those with me, and awoke feeling deeply distressed.

There is another that ought to be included; perhaps it is even the most relevant. It was a long dream in several sections, dealing specifically with someone who had formerly been trained as a Yogi, retaining considerable power in the life of today. I thought it related to my mother. The dream concluded in a different vein and a modern setting — a dim upper room where several persons were gathered. In the centre of the room stood a figure, hazy, in some way veiled — whose face I could not see. I heard a voice gently speaking, and listened intently. The intonation deepened, and my senses became alert. Suddenly the veil dissolved, features appeared, and the figure leapt into colour. I saw a white Indian turban, dark eyes, a strong nose and full mouth, and as I watched, astounded — recognition dawned. The voice became real to me; known, and deeply loved.

It was my Master! I *knew* it was my Master, and heard myself repeating "Master, Master, Master!" over and over again as I awoke.

He hears the lowly, suppliant voice
of the heart; he knows
when the heart's secret rises up to him.
When supplication opens the door of the heart,
what is desired comes forth to meet it;
The answering cry, 'Here I am!' of the friend
goes out to welcome the heart's 'O my Lord!'
rising up from the highway of submission.

Hakim Sanai, 'The Walled Garden of Truth', translated by David Pendlebury. Octagon Press Ltd. 1974 p. 42.

Feeling tired, bored, unhappy and utterly useless — on impulse one afternoon I telephoned Alison and asked her if there would be a T.S. meeting that evening. She said yes, the long holiday recess was now over, in fact the Lodge had met last Thursday while she was still away.

I had ventured to the Lodge one evening at the end of July, and found it as disappointing as ever, save for one woman (a newcomer) who recounted a 'memory' from a former incarnation of a house that was later confirmed as having existed. I hoped she would be there again.

Without any real enthusiasm I went. The date was September 13th 1962, and I had reached my lowest physical ebb for a very long time. The elderly couple who were the backbone of the Lodge were already present, Alison also — she smiled as I entered and settled myself down, and said she must introduce me to the Indian gentleman who was likewise a visitor to the Lodge this evening — I noticed then a dark-haired young man sitting behind the still open door. He was short, cheerful and smiling — giving a vague impression of all-over light brown, for his skin was fair for an Indian's, and his suit of a brownish material. He rose to his feet and beamed at me, proffering his outstretched hand — his beautiful brown eyes shining with amusement and friendliness. His name, he said, was Inder Sain, but please to call him Inder...

In such manner he introduced me to my destiny.

continued in Book II, 'BELOVED EXECUTIONER'.

Scheduled for Publication in August 1984:

BELOVED EXECUTIONER

by Kate Thomas.

Book 2 of the author's autobiographical trilogy, recording in detail her personal contact with a Sufi Teaching Master, and the mundane, psychological, and spiritual effects that resulted from this relationship.

A moving record of aspiration and endurance, outlining significant modes of perception and applied experience as yet unpublicised in the Western world.

ROSEKING PUBLICATIONS
P.O. Box 13. Cambridge CB4 1EZ
England.

First published in 1983. 154 pages.

APPROACH TO REALITY

by A.J. Peterson.

Many aspects of the requirements and effects of spiritual development are still little known in the West. This book attempts to describe the essential relationship between pupil and Teaching Master, also to outline some of the states experienced by a student of the Sufi Way.

The author's search for spiritual understanding leads him stage by stage through a series of occultly determined events involving eventually an intensely personal catharsis.

In the background is the enigmatic figure of Idries Shah, the Sufi Exemplar, whose precise and powerful teaching techniques are for the first time clearly illustrated in operation.

A book replete with psychological perception, spiritual observations and a searching interchange with the paranormal.

Hardback £9.50 Paperback £4.95
post free from

ROSEKING PUBLICATIONS.
P.O. Box 13. Cambridge CB4 1EZ
England.

ZONE 13

Ou
of the
Fog

CW01623718

David Orme

Text © David Orme, 1998

The right of David Orme to be identified as author of this work has been asserted by him in accordance with the Copyright, Designs and Patents Act 1988.

Text illustrations by Dave Bowyer
Cover illustration by Mark Duffin

All rights reserved. No part of this publication may be reproduced or transmitted in any form or by any means, electronic or mechanical, including photocopy, recording or any information storage and retrieval system, without permission in writing from the publisher or under licence from the Copyright Licensing Agency Limited. Further details of such licences (for reprographic reproduction) may be obtained from the Copyright Licensing Agency Limited of 90 Tottenham Court Road, London W1P 0LP.

First published in 1998 by
Stanley Thornes Publishers Ltd
Ellenborough House
Wellington Street
Cheltenham
GL50 1YW

99 00 01 02 03 \ 10 9 8 7 6 5 4 3 2

A catalogue record for this book is available from the British Library

ISBN 0-7487-3618-2

Typeset by Tech-Set Ltd., Gateshead

Printed and bound in Great Britain by T.J. International Ltd., Padstow, Cornwall

CONTENTS

1

FOG AT THE COTTAGE

The fog lay thick on the fields and marshes. It was like a white wall. Judy and Ben looked out of the cottage window. They couldn't even see the trees at the bottom of the garden.

"Why did Dad want to come and live in a place like this?" groaned Ben.

"You've said that a hundred times already," said Judy.

"I know, but why did he?"

Judy and Ben were staying with their father. Their parents had split up. They usually lived with their mother in her flat in London. They had come to spend a week with Dad in his cottage in Essex. They both thought it was the most boring place in the world. It was miles from the nearest town. Even the village was a long walk away.

Dad came in from the kitchen.

"What do you want to do today?"

Dad was an artist. He painted pictures of sea birds. The cottage was perfect for him. Outside were mud flats stretching out to the sea. They were covered in birds, but today you couldn't see them. You couldn't see anything.

"I wanted to go down to the village shop," said Judy. "But we can't go in this."

"Why not?" said Dad. "As long as you stick to the road, you can't get lost."

Ben and Judy put on their coats. Anything was better than sitting indoors.

2

THE EMPTY CAR

It was hard work walking back from the village. Dad had remembered that they were out of food and had given them a long shopping list. They had to carry four big bags of shopping home. They seemed to get heavier and heavier.

"Dad's really mean," said Judy. "He could have brought us in the car."

The fog wasn't quite so thick now. There was a wind, and the sun was trying to shine.

They saw something ahead of them on the road.

"It's a car!"

"It's Dad's car. He's come to meet us."

The car was by the side of the road. Its lights were on. The driver's door was open. The car radio was playing.

There was no sign of Dad.

They walked round to the driver's side. There was a terrible smell.

"What on earth is that stink?"

They both stared in alarm. There was smelly slime all over the road by the car door. It made a trail leading towards the sea.

It looked as if a giant slug had gone that way.

3

THE WRECK

"Something horrible has got Dad!" shouted Ben. "Come on!"

They dumped the shopping in the car and started to follow the stinking trail.

The fog was still lifting. The wind was pushing it out to sea. They ran over the shingle beach. The trail was easy to follow.

"Look!"

Ben was pointing ahead. In the distance,

they could see two figures. One of them was carrying a body over its shoulder.

"Dad!" Judy whispered.

It was getting difficult to follow the two figures now. The sand was turning to mud. Judy and Ben were wearing trainers, and they sank down at every footstep.

"Look at their footprints!" whispered Ben. "They've got feet like ducks!"

The creatures that had taken Dad didn't

look like ducks. They were tall, and upright like people. But their footprints were like ducks' feet – only much bigger.

"Webbed feet!" said Judy. "That's how they can walk across the mud!"

Ben peered ahead.

"I know where we are now. It's the wreck!"

They had seen the wreck before. They could see it from the windows of the cottage. It was an old barge.

Years ago, it had been left to rust away on the mud flats. The creatures were heading for the wreck.

What were they going to do to Dad when they got there?

4

JUST IN TIME

The creatures disappeared into the wreck. A minute later, they came out again – without Dad! They turned and headed across the mud towards the sea.

"Come on, Ben. We've got to try and get inside that wreck!"

It was very difficult. The mud was even deeper now. It seemed to be trying to suck off their shoes. Judy nearly lost hers twice. To make it worse, the tide was coming in. The channels were filling up with water. They remembered that the wreck was covered with water at high tide.

At last, they got to the wreck. One end of it was rusted right away. The other end still had a roof and sides. They saw a rusty door.

The door was hard to open. The handle was slippery with slime. They managed to get the door open by pulling together. A terrible smell, even worse than the slime, poured out.

Light came in through a hole in the deck above. Three shapes were lying on the floor. One of them was moving. It was Dad!

Ben and Judy looked at the other two shapes, then wished they hadn't. They were both human beings, but they had been in the sea a long time. They were white and swollen. Parts of their faces had been eaten away.

They both held their breath and tried not to

look at the bodies. They lifted Dad out into the open. He was tied up with bands of tough, jelly-like stuff. One band covered his mouth.

Ben found a loose piece of rusty iron. He managed to cut through the jelly with it. Dad seemed OK.

"Thank goodness you two came along! The tide was coming in fast. Another few minutes and I would have drowned in there!"

They started back across the mud. It was

getting even more difficult to walk.

"What are those creatures? What were those bodies doing in the wreck?"

"I've no idea," said Dad. "Whatever kind of creatures they are, I nearly ended up as their dinner! I thought of you struggling home with the shopping. I decided I would come and give you a lift. When I saw two figures in the fog, I stopped because I thought it was you. I suppose that wreck is where the creatures keep their food. They capture people, then leave them to drown and rot. Then they come back and eat them!"

Ben, Judy and Dad struggled on through the mud.

Behind them, they heard a sound. They turned.

The two creatures were following them.

5

BACK AT THE CAR

They were nearly at the shingle beach. If the creatures had caught them in the mud, they wouldn't have been able to escape.

"Quick!" yelled Dad. "Back to the car!"

They rushed up the beach. The creatures were getting closer. Ben, Judy and Dad got to the car and jumped in. They slammed and locked the doors. Dad tried to start the engine – but nothing happened!

"The battery's flat!" groaned Dad. "I left the lights on!"

The two creatures were by the car now. The three people inside could see them clearly. They were human in shape. Their skin was grey and slimy, like a slug's. They had huge, fish-like eyes and two holes instead of a nose.

One of them picked up a heavy stone from the beach. It started to smash the car windows with it.

Judy remembered something they had bought in the village. It was a bottle of bleach, with a spray top. She grabbed it and squirted the bleach through the broken window. It went right into the eyes of the creatures.

They both screamed. Judy watched in horror as their eyes started to melt away. They staggered over the road.

A lorry was coming the other way. With a

thud, it ran over both the creatures. They lay still, just a slimy mess on the road.

Later that night, six creatures came up out of the sea, and stood looking at what was left of their friends.

With anger in their huge eyes, they turned and headed for the cottage.